THE
PASSIONATE
ORGANIZATION

THE PASSIONATE ORGANIZATION

Igniting the Fire of Employee Commitment

James R. Lucas

AMACOM

American Management Association

New York • Atlanta • Boston • Chicago • Kansas City • San Francisco • Washington, D.C.
Brussels • Mexico City • Tokyo • Toronto

This publication is designed to provide accurate and authoritative information in regard to the subject matter covered. It is sold with the understanding that the publisher is not engaged in rendering legal,
accounting, or other professional service. If legal advice or other expert
assistance is required, the services of a competent professional person
should be sought.

Library of Congress Cataloging-in-Publication Data

Lucas, J. R. (James Raymond), 1950–
    The passionate organization : igniting the fire of employee commitment /
James R. Lucas.
      p.   cm.
    Includes bibliographical references and index.
    ISBN 0-8144-0477-4
    1. Organizational   effectiveness. 2. Employee   motivation. 3. Knowledge
workers.   4. Commitment (Psychology)   5. Organizational learning
6. Corporate culture.   I. Title.
HD58.9.L853   1999
658.3'14—dc21   98-54184
                                                                          CIP

Printing number

10   9   8   7   6   5   4

For
Laura Christine

Contents

Acknowledgments

Many thanks to the passionate people with whom I have worked over the years—people who have taught me a great deal about what it means to be passionate in a passion-destroying world. Their personal triumph has become a passionate triumph for their organizations.

Special thanks to my wonderful assistant, Janette Jasperson, for all of her excellent and devoted work on this, our third leadership book together in three years. It is a better book because she brought her knowledge and passion to bear on it. As always, my deep appreciation to my daughter Laura for her input. I am grateful to Priscilla Buchanan for her efforts and encouragement. And my thanks to Tom Brown, Rick Graham, John Hughes, Walt Lantzy, Philip Lewis, Hunter Lott, and Michael Mahoney for their insights.

I also want to thank the many people with whom I have gotten to share ideas in my work as a consultant, speaker, and seminar leader. This includes my friends and colleagues at the American Management Association, American Society for Training and Development, Astra USA, Black & Veatch, Broadman & Holman, Creative Leadership Strategies, Enlightened Leadership International, Hallmark, Harley-Davidson, Hewlett-Packard, Jones Apparel, Occupations Inc., Pinnacle Resources, PricewaterhouseCoopers, Sprint, and VF Corporation. I especially want to thank the Vision Team that is passionately building a new future for an old company, Potlatch Corporation: Val Ahrens, Chuck Appelholm, Gale Berg, David Betts, Scott Dean, John Dunn, Jeff Fisher, Jon Gardiner, Gordon Haines, Coni Hammond, Karl Hedley, Tom Isle, Lee Johnson, Tim Krohn, Aubrey Lipford, Jack Moseley, Bryan Palmer, Jimmy Roberson, Steve Roberson, Margi Sloan, Larry Streeby, Mike Sullivan, Mike Wallace, team sponsor John Bacon, President Penn Siegel, and CEO John Richards for his insight and fore-sight. I hope you all never lose the fire.

This is also my third leadership book in three years with my ex-cellent editor at AMACOM, Adrienne Hickey. Her passion for the concept of this book and its contents have made it a better and more enjoyable project. I also very much appreciate the invaluable input on the manuscript from Niels Buessem. And I don't know if the detailed editing process should be fun, but Shelly Wert, my Associate Editor, made it so.

Thanks to my family for their understanding and support. Watching me work for three years in a row was quite a challenge. Their passion for what I was doing helped make the project even more worthwhile and exciting for me, as I watched them live out the principles in this book.

Finally, my thanks to S.M. for all of your inspiration and encouragement.

Introduction

Heart Over Head

Nothing ever succeeds which exuberant spirits have not helped to produce.

—Georg Wilhelm Nietzsche, *The Twilight of the Gods*

Top-flight performance is not dry and deadly; it is spirited, it is emotion-filled.

—Tom Peters and Nancy Austin, *A Passion for Excellence*

If you can give your son or daughter only one gift, let it be enthusiasm.

—Bruce Barton, American ad man and politician

The "old reliables" are all gone.

Technical superiority. Product features and benefits. Service enhancements. World-class quality. Economies of scale. Control of raw materials and proprietary processes. Even the value of a household name ("branding") and a good reputation. These competitive advantages, which once were (and in some cases still are) erroneously thought to be sustainable, are being ground into dust by a global economy that laughs at them. Even globalization has turned out to be no panacea; being a major player in someone else's collapsing economy, as Coca-Cola, Gillette, and others have found, can mean that our hard-won position simply erodes our profits on a grander scale.

And now, reason itself has joined the list of casualties.

The entire Industrial Revolution was based on reason. Division of labor, economies of scale, and interchangeable parts were the rational organization's inheritance from the Enlightenment of the eighteenth and early nineteenth centuries. Machine-driven, people-as-cogs production—honed to logical perfection by the "scientific management" of Frederick Taylor—was the gift of the late nineteenth and early twentieth centuries. Then came the rational organization of the mid- to late twentieth century, with everything structured and codified—organization charts, process charts, career paths, job descriptions, policy manuals, finely detailed procedures.

A to B to C. It's all there in black and white. Anyone can trace anything into the past and extrapolate anything into the future. It's an engineer's dream. Part of my background is in engineering, and I love it.

Strategic planning and the learning organization are the capstones of these centuries of rational direction that have produced so much wealth, created a huge middle class, and allowed our freedom to have tangible expression. There have been many abuses, because progress is not nearly as neat as the rational model would suggest, but all in all it has been a pretty fine ride for humanity.

And now the capstones are cracking and leaking.

Strategic planning—preparing for the future more intelligently than our competitors—has been the most recent competitive advantage to disappear. Its demise stems in part from the fact that everyone is doing it, and in part from its inherent flaws and limitations. Henry Mintzberg, Gary Hamel, and others have clearly documented the fallacies and futility of traditional strategic and rational planning in a turbulent world full of dramatic change, relentless competitors, and economic surprises.[1] The fall of the Soviet Union, an empire built around planning—with the ultimate supporting tool of totalitarian power to enforce it—is the exclamation point at the end of the era of planning that began with the Industrial Revolution and went into high gear after World War II.

And so we have entered the postindustrial age, the age of learning, the day of the "knowledge worker." It has been said that the only sustainable competitive advantage is the ability to learn faster than our competitors. This has rightly produced an intensive drive to build learning/teaching organizations, as evidenced by the 1,200 organizations that have created "corporate universities" since 1988.[2] But once again, we may have fallen prey to the rational model—the conviction not only that knowledge is power but that knowledge is enough.

It isn't enough. A disorganized start-up destroys a textbook organizational masterpiece. People who don't even know how to write a business plan eat the lunch of people with degrees in business and planning. An uneducated revolutionary annihilates an entrenched, well-oiled bureaucracy.

Thinking and planning aren't dead. They're just not *enough*. And they have definitely become secondary in the face of the onslaught of exciting and terrifying newness. The learning organization will, in the years to come, fade from primary favor like its rational predecessor, strategic planning, as the linchpin of success.

We don't *have* to replace these theories. We can continue to try to make them work. But in the end our efforts will fail. These theories will give us pleasant illusions for a while, with their detail and their decimal points and their measurements of intellectual capital. But the illusions will fade in the harsh glow of reality. These theories are secondary—and if we're not careful, they'll become gigantic red herrings.

What can supersede strategic and rational planning? For heaven's sake, what can top the learning organization?

Passion.

Passion can help us make shifts and leaps that strategic planning can neither envision nor imagine. Planning must give way— and in some leading organizations has already begun to give way—to an ongoing, fiery discussion among people who care. The process, the ritual, has become impotent, a bow and arrow against a cannon-laden future.

And passion is *even more* fundamental than the learning organization, because it is passion that gives us the driving reason to learn and to apply our new knowledge effectively. Ultimately, we are driven not by what we *know* but by what we *feel*. Learning is important, even critical, but it is of highest value only when it supports and extends our passion.

Why? Because passionate people think with their hearts as well as their heads. They don't have to think "out of the box" because they've never been *in* the box in the first place. They fight for ideas they believe in and won't be shut up by plans and procedures. They chafe under the command to "be reasonable." They'll continue to press for projects that will be the future of the organization long after logic has declared them dead. They'll learn from mistakes and won't let failures dim their enthusiasm to keep trying.

The passionate organization will beat the big organization, the cash-rich organization, the savvy organization, and—yes—even the learning organization. The passionate organization—which can exist only when composed almost exclusively of passionate people focused on a common vision—can alone bring the breakthroughs, the continuous improvement, the creativity, and the innovation to succeed big and demolish bored and boring foes. "Passion persuades," says Anita Roddick, founder of The Body Shop. "If I had to nominate a driving force in my life, I'd pump for passion every time."

Only the passion of every person involved with our organization will be able to keep us alive and out in front. Even one passionless person in our midst saps our corporate life and puts us at a disadvantage to the truly passionate organization. To thrive, we have to guard access to our organizational life force.

The organization that wins in the twenty-first century will focus its attention on passion. It will find, develop, and articulate a vision for which all of its people will be willing to fight long and hard. It will only hire people who are passionate by nature, and especially passionate about its vision. It will methodically and quickly cut out the deadwood—including the really smart people who don't *believe.* At the same time, it will prize originality and feistiness and diversity and even the offbeat, and it will loathe the status quo and "one best way" and things that look like everything else. It will emphasize inspiring vision, big purpose, deeply-held core values, mutual trust, and stretch goals more than planning and learning.

A point of clarification: This is most assuredly *not* a book on how to "motivate" employees. And this is not a book on how to have "fun" in the workplace (although passionate organizations can be deeply enjoyable places to work). There are no schemes or gimmicks or programs here. Rather, this is a book on how to build a truly passionate organization—how to ignite a fire of commitment in the core of who we are as people, how to use that fire to create a living future, and how to be on the winning side when the enthusiasm of the heart overwhelms the logic of the head.

It is difficult to maintain our balance when we're at the cutting edge. We need people who can do more, people who can find a way to wield the cutting edge. And we need an organizational life that will support them in this dynamic action.

We have arrived at an interesting crossroads in organizational development. In the midst of an incredibly complex world, the formula for organizational survival and success has become surprisingly simple: passion.

The choice is between the passion of all our people, all the time, or death—the death of our vision, the death of our goals, the death of our legacy, and probably the death of our organization.

We can make the right choice.

Notes

1. See especially Henry Mintzberg's book *The Rise and Fall of Strategic Planning* (New York: The Free Press, 1994).
2. Survey, *USA Today*, July 13, 1998.

Part I

Passion Over Knowledge

We can't talk about passionate people or passionate organizations without first talking about passion.

We will lead off by defining passion—what it is and what it isn't. We will talk about the necessity for passion in a world where reason is limited, both in its usefulness and in its value as a competitive advantage.

We will take time to analyze two tools of reason that organizations are relying on to win, but that *aren't enough:* strategic planning and the learning organization. While they are good tools, they are inadequate foundations for success.

We will close the first section with an overview of the dynamic—and often scary—direction that passionate organizations will take.

Passion can be squelched, but it can't be beaten. Passion can't be quantified, but it can be released.

1

Defining Passion

Life is too short to be little. Man is never so manly as when he feels deeply, acts boldly, and expresses himself with frankness and with fervour.

—Benjamin Disraeli, *Coningsby*

It is not enough to fight. It is the spirit which we bring to the fight that decides the issue. It is morale that wins the victory.

—George Catlett Marshall, *Military Review*

We *are* born to glow. We aspire to it. We yearn for it. We dread long periods without it. We curse what blocks it. We embrace all that animates it. We wither when it's lost. We flourish when it's found. A life lacking glow is mere existence—no, *less*.

—Tom Brown, *The Anatomy of Fire*

We want to know the way.

We're looking for a formula, a process, a checklist, an idea—or maybe just an encouragement that we can, in fact, achieve success in the exciting, ferocious, staring-us-in-the-face third millennium.

It's only natural that we would look to our rational selves for the answers. It's only—well, logical. We love step-by-step guides and formulas. The simpler and more orderly and logical, the better. It sounds like . . . a plan.

But it isn't enough. It isn't even the place to start. In the world in which we are actually living, whether we like it or not, the rational, formulaic approach won't produce results of the same magnitude as our challenges.

The most turbulent marketplace of all is the marketplace of ideas. And the reality is that strategic planning can't anticipate the direction of this newest incarnation of the free market, and the learning organization can't conquer it.

If we want to be successful in the next century, we will have to go deeper than the rational planning model that underpins so much of strategic planning and learning organization thinking. As author Tom Peters says, "Crazy times call for crazy organizations." These crazy organizations will have to go to the nonrational (as opposed to irrational) core, passion and emotion, that drives what, how much, and how well we learn, respond, and innovate.

The Nature of Positive Passion

"Intense or violent emotion . . . a great liking or enthusiasm." So says Webster's about passion. It goes on to define a passionate person as one "easily moved to strong emotion; showing or inspired by strong emotion . . . intense." Intensity is the living opposite of what we find in most organizations, where putting in time and playing staid office politics are the norm.

Passion versus putting in time. You can feel the difference—in a waiter, a hotel registration clerk, a cabbie, a flight attendant, a salesperson, an employee, a supervisor. Some people have the aroma of life—they're excited, full of energy, and glad to be doing whatever they're doing. Others have had all the life drained out of them. They've let the "fire in the belly" turn into "gripes in the guts" (an old colonial expression) or go out altogether.

We all have moods and bad days. But some of us, regardless of the difficulty of our circumstances, choose to have passion at our core. We *choose* to be passionate, to be intense, to care, to fight. True passion is always more of a choice than a feeling.

There's nothing like passion. One untrained but passionate novice, given a little time and some resources and encouragement, will rise above any ten trained but dispassionate experts as surely as the passionate upstart organization will bring its rational entrenched competitors to their knees.

There are, to be sure, different types of passion. Some of the positive passions are:

- *Zest for life.* This is the joyous passion for simply being alive. Most children have it, and then life and processes (familial, educational, social, organizational) begin to squeeze it out. Add in a few bad decisions—college and career choices, friends and spouses—and whatever passion has managed to survive the childhood passion-crushing juggernaut will seep away. Passionate adults are often considered to be eccentrics or worse. The few who hang onto their zest for life have a tremendous edge on the mass of rational and irrational people around them, but they won't always feel that this is so. They may feel odd, except when they feel really good. "I used to think that anyone doing anything weird was weird," said songwriter Paul McCartney. "I suddenly realized that anyone doing anything weird wasn't weird at all and it was the people saying they were weird that were weird."

- *Drive to accomplish.* This is the passion we feel when we are well matched with the work we are doing—when our talents and interests coincide with those required by the job. Most people aren't matched up very well at all. But when someone is, get out of the way. The performance—and the related learning—will skyrocket. Accomplishment is both oversold and undersold in our time. Accomplishment at all costs, no; but accomplishment as a thing of beauty, as a contribution to a sense of purpose and being, as a point on the way to leaving a legacy, yes.

- *Competitive fire.* This is the passion we feel when we are fighting to win. The best place for this to start is with ourselves, as we compete against our own previous best, our standards, and our entropy and tendency to slack off. Healthy competition against others, inside and outside our organization, can be of benefit. Competing against the difficult or impossible is another whole level of fierceness. And if we have an enemy to fight against, so much the better. Big hairy audacious goals are good. Big hairy audacious enemies may be even better.

- *Passion for truth.* Ultimately, the main passion that pays big dividends is the passion for truth. This involves an almost desperate desire to see and know and understand, and, most important of all, to face and accept reality. It senses that the only way to lead a passionately effective life is to build it on the truth, whether that is personal truth (really knowing ourselves), relational truth, or marketplace truth. It is the quest itself that keeps the discovered truth from turning hard-bitten or cynical. It is a passion that knows that success is rooted in both reality and optimism, and seeks to become a pragmatic dreamer, a realistic optimist.

Thomas Jefferson, the "American Leonardo," embodied all of these different types of positive passion. Perhaps the greatest thinker of the Enlightenment, he was also a mass of passions and emotions and contradictions (both real and apparent). His zest for life spanned decades and continents. His drive to accomplish spurred him to lead both a revolution and the invention of a new form of government. His competitive drive pressed him to positions as secretary of state, vice president, and two-term president of the United States, as well as to the doubling in size of the nation. And his passion for truth lead him to the three great acts he noted on his tombstone: the Declaration of Independence (which still stirs the soul), the Virginia Statutes of Religious Freedom, and the founding of the University of Virginia.

Jefferson was not a perfect man. Jeffersonians wince when they think about his resistance to freeing, and dealing with, his own slaves. But even with regard to slavery he was passionate in spirit. In 1769, he authored a bill for the Virginia House of Burgesses, an audience of slaveholders he had to know would oppose him violently, that would have taken the first step toward abolishing slavery in Virginia. Even in his first draft of the Declaration of Independence, he included a bold proposal to abolish the slave trade. "What is most significant about Thomas Jefferson is that he wrote the Declaration of Independence," says black American writer Albert Murray. "So the basis for rejecting or struggling against slavery has been laid in the social contract by Thomas Jefferson. There was no such basis in Africa or any other place. . . . Thomas Jefferson gives you the basis for the struggle for your humanity and for human dignity, [though] he had some contradictions in his life."[1]

The Power of Passion

Few writings better capture the power of passion as compared with reason than Jefferson's simple "Dialogue Between My Head and My Heart," in which his heart, speaking to his head, points out the head's limitations. Jefferson, the great rationalist and supreme product of the

Enlightenment, saw reason's limitations and the power of passion in the very creation of the United States:

> If our country, when pressed with wrongs at the point of the bayonet, had been governed by its heads instead of its hearts, where should we have been now? hanging on a gallows as high as Haman's. You began to calculate and to compare wealth and numbers: we threw up a few pulsations of our warmest blood: we supplied enthusiasm against wealth and numbers: we put our existence to the hazard, when the hazard seemed against us, and we saved our country.[2]

Passion is so powerful because we learn and plan based on reason, but we move and change and achieve based on passion. While reason affects our mind, passion affects our emotions and spirituality—how we feel about things, how these things relate to our being and destiny. We can learn and plan, plan and learn, but without passion, we will ultimately shrivel and die.

We have, for several centuries, correctly elevated the rational over the irrational. The superstitions and falsities of the preceding era were rightly dissected and discarded in the healthy glow of the Enlightenment. But very early on, some people recognized that perceiving the world as only rational or irrational was too limited. Beginning with the Romantic movement of the early nineteenth century, artists, composers, and authors brought to the fore another dimension of human behavior: the nonrational.

The nonrational is our unseen core. The nonrational is the deepest and best part of who we are and what our organizations can become. The order looks like this:

Nonrational (positive passion) → Rational (dispassionate) → Irrational (negative passion)

The nonrational drives us. It is anchored to and checked by the rational. We use our reason to aid us in achieving our dreams. And the power of our passions keeps cold-blooded reason from sinking into its opposite, irrationality.

The nonrational is a person's or an organization's soul—our beliefs, values, interests, passions, and emotions. These aspects of our humanity give meaning to our thinking and learning—to the rational part of our lives. Without the soul, there would be no reason to learn. Once the connection between the nonrational and the rational is severed, once reason rules, the slide to irrationality—maybe slow, maybe fast—becomes our destiny. The rational German state of Hitler, so efficient in rebuilding the German economy and military, so insane in how it used them.

The Passionate Organization

Many writers have tried to define the key elements of successful organizations. A number of them have been summarized in Table 1-1 located at the end of this chapter. I have tried to place similar ideas on the same line, and have shown only the elements that appear in at least three of the four columns.

As Kevin Laverty, University of Washington professor of policy and strategy, says, "Explaining the success or failure of a business, while basic, is one of the greatest challenges in the study of business. For educators, the problem is to develop a model for success that can be described and communicated."[3] Although some of the elements in Table 1-1 might encourage passion, and some of them are what passionate people do, and in fact they are all terrific ideas, passion as a key is nowhere to be found. Perhaps a big part of the reason why these writers overlook passion is their focus on organizational structure and systems, the rational things we can do to be successful. (Tom Peters, to be sure, has since grabbed firmly onto the need for passion as a driving force, from *A Passion for Excellence* on.)

The bottom line is, who is going to do all of this stuff? Well-trained seals? Will it be the by-product of a well-designed and well-oiled machine? Can we count on it to happen, just because it *has* to happen if we are to survive and prosper?

Only a passionate organization, chock-full of mutually-committed people at all levels, will be able to accomplish the great and sometimes even noble ideas in the table.

When you walk into some organizations, you feel the emptiness of the interior climate: It's flat, dull, dead, boring, and bored. There's no fire. It's foolish to expect good numbers in the long run from this kind of organization. Even if the organization hits the numbers for a while, the resulting soul death is too high a price to pay for merely financial goals. In the best of these lifeless places, people are trained to impersonate passionate people. There may even be a policy manual or a training program that attempts to get the effect. But it won't matter, in the long run, to the customers or the employees. You can mimic passion for a while, but you can't fake it. People are just too damned smart.

But in other organizations, you can feel the fire. It's there, all the way down to the lowest levels in the organization. People care, they seem to be in the know, they somehow seem smarter than the dead-heads in the dead-end organizations. Passion almost always makes people seem smarter.

Why? Knowledge is difficult to acquire when we don't really care about it or how it can be used. Even if we're well read—even if we're in a learning organization, if we're not passionate about what we're learning, the information is eviscerated and will become value-less. We may rely on it, entrench ourselves in it, even defend it, but it's unlikely that we'll fight or die for it.

The list of knowledge-rich organizations that have failed to capitalize on their knowledge is long and should give us pause:

- The personal computer was invented by Xerox, which shoved it off to the side and turned it over to competitors, actually teaching a passionate Steve Jobs everything the company knew.

- IBM had the dominant position in the world of computers, but missed the power of the PC the first time around, then took its fiery new division and subordinated it to the dinosaur of the mainframe business. IBM had sufficient knowledge to develop and control both the software and hardware sides of the new industry, but instead allowed passionate upstarts like Microsoft and Intel to blow past it.

- The U.S. government has watched the collapse of governmental planning all over the world, from the total-control (read: silly and disastrous) planning of the totalitarian monstrosities like the Soviet Union and its Eastern Bloc satellites, to the socialist planning of Western nations like France, to the partnership "crony capitalism" planning of the "powerhouses" of Asia. Our own history shows the effectiveness of the opposite policy: free-market democracy based on the rule of law. We've seen the good things that happen when government-regulated monopolies (read: stupid, inefficient, arrogant) are broken up, as happened with the airlines, the telecommunications industry, and transportation. But, no matter: Many leaders in

Washington, D.C., have no passion to use the vast and easily accessible pool of knowledge gleaned from our own history and the experiences of others. Their passion, in great part, is for power and influence, not for the legacy of a better world and a freer people.

What Passion Is Not

Everything casts a shadow, and passion is no exception. As we look at passion in this book, we need to agree on what it *isn't* or should not be.

• *Passion isn't acting without thinking.* Passion does not replace reason. Passion without thinking can be an error-filled charging bull. We want our passions to prioritize our thinking, and we want to stay away from sterile thinking devoid of any passion, but we do want our reason to guide and inform our passion.

• *Passion isn't spontaneity without purpose.* "Try a lot of stuff and keep what works," is a business mantra that contains both a truth and a misdirection. No organization would be what it is today if it had limited itself to the letter of its prior strategic plans. We do have to test, try out, experiment, but not just for the sake of seeking out new things. There has to be a purpose behind our experimentation. Might this new direction even remotely advance us toward our vision? Might it possibly please our customers? Passion without purpose is frivolous.

• *Passion isn't fervor without clarity.* Passion doesn't mean fighting for causes we don't even understand. We let our passions drive us, but then we stop for a while to add up the scores and see where we might be going astray. Reason can be a useful tool to check and balance very active passions.

• *Passion isn't intuition and "gut feel."* Passion is not an excuse to avoid doing the hard work of thinking. We may have a great idea and be ready to put it into play; our gut says, "Go." But we do ourselves a disservice if we don't bring all that we are, including our best rational selves, to bear on the decision. The challenge, of course, is to keep reason from killing whatever it can't understand or explain.

• *Passion isn't perversity.* Newscasters talk about "crimes of passion." I've seen tyrannical managers call their uncontrolled rage "just being honest." We are not speaking of the passions that destroy, the irrational passions, the negative passion.

Negative Passion

Negative passion can cause knowledge to be obscured, ignored, or even contorted. When the rational is cut off from the nonrational— when knowledge isn't rooted in a fundamental, positive, clear vision and values—the dispassionate rational will sink into a morass of negative irrationality that will in time devour the knowledge.

Negative passion uses inner power and energy (and acquired knowledge) in destructive ways: tearing down others, obstructing new directions, fighting for a bad cause. Zeal can be misused and can cause incredible damage. At the global level, it can lead nations to build nuclear weapons when they haven't even discovered basic sanitation, and to create self-immolating policies that restrict trade, misdirect resources, and attempt to control prices and wages. Negative passion is irrational because it is usually counterproductive (at least in the long run) to the negative person's own life and career. If I have to have an enemy, let him be cold-blooded rational rather than hot-blooded irrational.

Passion is the driving force that determines how we will use knowledge. A positive passion can use knowledge in an effective way. It can elevate that knowledge to a place where it can improve the lot of many people. And negative passion? It can use knowledge for ill-begotten purposes:

- Knowledge about psychology can be used to dominate and control others and force them into passiveness and dependency.
- Knowledge about sociology and politics can be used to play territorial games and wage territorial wars.
- Inside knowledge about other departments and divisions can be used to keep people off balance and to build personal empires.
- Knowledge about people's fears can be used to squeeze more and more out of them, including actions that go against their convictions. The secret of Bob Dole's success as the majority

leader of the U.S. Senate was that he never used his influence to persuade people to vote against their convictions.

- Knowledge of people's weaknesses and needs is routinely used by the selfish and unscrupulous to lure others into schemes and bad relationships.
- Knowledge of people's expectations can cause organizational leaders to hone their message so that it apparently meets those expectations, and to spin their results so that it looks like they are hitting the expectations, even when they know there is no way they can do so. Sometimes, the spins are prepared at the same time as the original message.
- Knowledge of customers can be used to pad prices, push phony charges through incompetent bureaucracies, and sell products, services, and specifications that the customers don't need and wouldn't buy if the playing field were level.
- Knowledge of suppliers can be used to make unfair demands, dump inventory problems on them, and slash their pricing.
- Knowledge about competitors can be used to steal their ideas, void their patents, misuse alliances, and wreck the careers and lives of people whom we've never met but who are very, very real.
- Knowledge of the legal process can lead organizations to strike first and turn the other party into a "defendant" for years to come. And the problem isn't just lawyers, who in many ways are just a reflection of the "I'm going to get you" attitude that way too many people carry around inside.

The irony is that negative passion can be encouraged by organizations that stress the rational without a nonrational foundation. "Do it because it's logical and reasonable" can lead to extremely efficient genocide of "undesirables," complete with continuous improvement in processes and methods. "Do it because it's right and generous" can lead to caring and sacrifice for those very same "undesirables." If we stress hitting certain revenue numbers in a certain time frame to our salespeople, they may lie to customers, overcommit, or run up sales on less profitable (or even unprofitable) products. If instead we nurture a passion for feeling customers' pain, anticipating their needs, perceiving their unmet needs, and offering solutions to their problems, it is unlikely that the salespeople's focus will deteriorate to irrationality.

We will look in a later chapter at ways to transform and eliminate these negative passions as much as possible in day-to-day organizational life.

The Absence of Passion

There are organizations that seem passionless, neither fired up to add value nor fired up to subtract it. "We may affirm absolutely that nothing great in the world has ever been accomplished without passion," observed Friedrich Wilhelm Hegel. But many organizations try to survive without it.

Where do these machines come from? In a sense, they are the products of the rational organization. The "ideal" (everything planned, no deviations, "spontaneity not welcome here") can lead directly to the absence of passion. Dispassion can even become the honored result: "We do things around here by the book." Passion is wrung out of the system and discarded as a distraction.

In the long run, these passionless, rationalistic robots will drift into irrationality and its corresponding negative passions. They'll become like General Motors, the dream machine of Alfred Sloan, with its entrenched methods, almost incapable of not shooting itself in the foot.

And there are those, and hopefully there will be more, who survey the cold, rational landscape and say, "It's not enough." Like Data, the ultimately logical but emotion-seeking android of *Star Trek,* they begin the long search for fire.

Conclusion

Charles Handy, philosopher and writer, once took a group of executives to a circus, where the performers displayed a sense of teamwork and trust that astonished his entourage. One said to him, "We pay people a quarter of a million pounds a year, and don't get that kind of stuff. What are we missing?" Handy's response? "Two things. One, they care passionately about what they do. Two, a thousand people stand and applaud after each of their performances. They have passion and pride and professionalism."[4]

Passion comes in many forms, and sometimes is even hard to see (although it is very hard to disguise over time). It can appear as

Table 1-1. Key Elements of Successful Organizations, as Identified by Influential Writers

Concept	In Search of Excellence by Thomas J. Peters and Robert H. Waterman, Jr.[a]	Built to Last: Successful Habits of Visionary Companies by James C. Collins and Jerry I. Porras[b]	The Eleven Commandments of 21st Century Management by Matthew J. Kiernon[c]	The 8 Practices of Exceptional Comapnies by Jac Fitz-Enz[d]
Remember that action beats endless deliberation.	A bias for action	Try a lot of stuff and keep what works.	Create a bias for speed and action in your company.	
Get everyone to think like business owners.	Autonomy and entrepreneurship		Get entrepreneurial and experimental	Competitive passion
Tap into people's skills to improve overall performance.	Productivity through people	Good enough never is.	Use all of your people, all of their skills, all of the time.	

Define your business and stay with it over time.	Stick to the knitting.	Clock building, not time telling		Commitment to a core strategy
Agree that purpose and results are more important than structures and systems.	Simple form, lean staff		Break internal and external barriers.	Collaboration
Utilize diverse and broad-based measurements of success.		More than profits	Develop strategic performance measurement tools.	Balanced value fixation

[a]Thomas J. Peters and Robert H. Waterman, Jr., *In Search of Excellence* (New York: Warner Books, 1982).
[b]James C. Collins and Jerry I. Porras, *Built to Last: Successful Habits of Visionary Companies* (New York: HarperBusiness, 1994).
[c]Matthew J. Kiernan, *The Eleven Commandments of 21st Century Management* (Englewood Cliffs, N.J.: Prentice-Hall, 1996).
[d]Jac Fitz-Enz, *The 8 Practices of Exceptional Companies* (New York: AMACOM Books, 1997).

dynamic enthusiasm, like a Celine Dion or a Winston Churchill. It can show itself as a relentless pursuit of excellence, like a Michael Jordan or a Jack Welch. It can become visible as wild energy, like a Jenna Elfman or a Groucho Marx. But whenever we see it, we know it, even if we don't understand it. And we want it. It's ours. It belongs to us.

We have been trained in many ways to believe that we cannot trust our emotions, and that it is folly to follow them. But our passions are the only things that make life interesting, and certainly the only things that lead to all-out efforts and worthwhile achievements. Leaders who find ways to design and enliven passionate organizations, and populate them with passionate people, will have the foundational key to success—short, medium, and long term.

Passion. There is no substitute for it, and nothing can imitate it over time. Create an environment full of passion, and when you compete with the strategically planned, rational learning organization, no matter how brilliant it is, you need not fear.

You will win.

Notes

1. As quoted in *Booknotes,* ed. Brian Lamb (New York: Times Books, 1997), p. 26.
2. As quoted in *The Portable Thomas Jefferson,* ed. Merrill D. Peterson (New York: The Viking Press, 1975), pp. 409–410.
3. Kevin J. Laverty, "Lessons from Microsoft: A Model for Strategy and Leadership." *Strategy & Leadership,* March/April 1996, p. 44.
4. As quoted in *Across the Board,* April 1998, p. 1.

2

The Limitations
of Reason

Man is only great when he acts from the passions; never irresistible but when he appeals to the imagination.

—Benjamin Disraeli, *Coningsby*

The first glance at History convinces us that the actions of men proceed from their needs, their passions, their characters and talents; and impresses us with the belief that such needs, passions and interests are the sole spring of actions.

—Georg Hegel, *The Philosophy of History*

Man is to be found in reason, God in the passions.

—G. C. Lichtenberg, *Aphorisms*

We need intelligent organizations.

The problem is that we define *intelligent* too narrowly. Does intelligent mean loaded with information? Rich with knowledge? Aware of its surroundings? Chock-full of patents and other intellectual property? Capable of sharing what it knows?

The answer to all of these is both "yes" and "not enough." These are bits and pieces of intelligence in an organization, but they are not the main or even the most important part.

Organizations that are truly intelligent will exhibit the same full range of intelligences that people at their best have and utilize. These include mental intelligence, emotional intelligence, and spiritual intelligence. Emotional and spiritual intelligence are in the realm of the nonrational, where passions live and are stirred.

Mental intelligence, expressed in our reasoning faculties, is extremely important. Although we will criticize what has become its worship, we will never deny its value and importance. But it is only a part of success—often the smallest part.

We hear a logical argument, but we are not moved to action. Why not? Because action is driven by our passions, not our reason. "The heart has its reasons, which reason knows not of," said French philosopher and mathematician Blaise Pascal. Misunderstanding this can be a deeply entrenched organizational disease masquerading as a cure. "[In 1981] business schools probably taught about GE more than any other company. The paradigm was that rational scientific management, devoid of passionate leadership, was the key to success."[1] It was Jack Welch's *abandonment* of this entrenched system that led to GE's becoming the world's most valuable company (market value, share price times number of shares outstanding) as of this writing.

Let's take a look at some of the key factors that limit the effectiveness of reason as a driving force for success.

The Role of Presuppositions

Often, when we think we are being rational, we are simply (and perhaps disastrously) basing our decisions on an assorted collection of beliefs, myths, assumptions, and prejudices. But then we "rationalize" our choices—which doesn't mean that we *make* them reasonable, but rather that we make them *seem* reasonable. Some examples:

• We tell everyone that the new hire was the best person for the job, when the reality is that we hired him because he reminded us of ourselves.

• We pick a certain checkout line because, we tell ourselves, it's "moving faster." The reality is that the checkout clerk is of our own race, or at least isn't of one of those "incompetent" races.

• We select a capital appropriations plan because we have been very successful in that area, and it is only logical to "stick to our knitting" and not "fix what ain't broke." The reality is that it is easier not to think, not to ask where our success may be sowing the seeds of our own de struction, and not to face the utterly reasonable fact that our mathematically precise predictions of the future are really lazy hopes in disguise.

• We select someone for a promotion because she has gone through a long and pertinent apprenticeship. What we really mean is that she has "paid her dues" and "deserves a shot," even though she may not be the right choice for the job. National political parties are forever doing this with really inadequate candidates, who have already reached their level of incompetence.

• We fire someone because he is a rabble-rouser, not a team player, a real pain in the neck who is destroying our sense of teamwork. It's really logical. The truth is that we don't like dealing with fire, with passion, with emotion, with disagreement, with creative conflict, with ambiguity, with things that aren't neat and tidy. As the Roman satirist Horace once said, "Men of sense fear to come in contact with a raging poet." Many great ideas are thus logically slaughtered.

• Perhaps the worst is our "logical" expectation that the future will be an extension and extrapolation of the past. We keep rejecting and resenting the "illogical" intrusion of reality—customer changes, market changes, value changes, process changes—even though all of these changes may be completely logical at their core.

In an interwoven and volatile global economy that is outside the control of any nation or group of nations, economic decisions and events in even obscure parts of the real world can cause market conditions to change suddenly and dramatically anywhere—or everywhere.

This last point is the Waterloo of presuppositions disguised as reason. Presuppositions are based on an assembled grid of perceptions that make up a whole "reality." "But perception isn't reality, reality is reality," says John Bacon, vice president of Potlatch Corporation. "If you perceive something that is different from reality, it's not perception, it's misunderstanding." But even where our perceptions are right on the mark, in the long run they can fail *because reality changes.*

For example, computer studies sponsored by the Club of Rome (a global think tank) around 1970 indicated that problems caused by overpopulation would devastate the world by the mid-1990s. What these studies failed to foresee was a dramatic decline in the birthrate in both industrialized and Third World countries. At the time of this writing, no country in Europe has a birthrate high enough to maintain its current population level. In fact, most developed countries may soon have a larger number of elderly people than can be supported by younger workers—the opposite problem to the one predicted by the Club of Rome. "What is happening now has simply never happened before in the history of the world," said Nicholas Eberstadt, a demographer based at the American Enterprise Institute in Washington.[2]

Reality isn't static. Even our accurate perceptions of reality can become inaccurate if we fix our perceptions in time and space.

It's far too easy to draw conclusions or make decisions based on presuppositions and then do a mental quick change to call our choice "reasonable."[3]

The only solution is to have a passion for truth, personally and organizationally, that can get beyond these often deeply entrenched presuppositions. It is the passion that listens rather than defends, changes rather than persists, and chucks the old when the new is better or "righter."

The Speculative Nature of Inductive Thinking

Most people in organizational life know only a portion of the data related to any given situation. Examples?

- The CEO looks like she is making a really dumb acquisition of a failing company, but we don't see that what she is really buying is two underappreciated patents.
- We hear that the management committee is shutting down a plant that has hit all of its production numbers with decent quality and a good safety record, and figure it's just another big downsizing to improve next quarter's numbers. But we don't hear about is that market's pricing, which has made every unit produced a financial loser.
- We see Tom fire Garrett, and assume it's because of the static Garrett always gave Tom during meetings. The reality is that Garrett was an abusive manager who destroyed morale in his department and, in the process, destroyed several effective people as well.

It is very, very hard to take small or limited facts and inductively generalize them into truly logical and reasonable conclusions. But that doesn't stop us from trying. Partly we're driven to do so by our human need to make sense of the world around us. But when we try to draw a universal conclusion from an infinitesimal sample of the whole realm of facts pertaining to an issue, the conclusion can be very skewed.

Two of our major customers complain. Sales of product "Y" sag 5 percent in one region. A competitor drops a portion of the same product line we are carrying. What does it mean? Maybe a lot. Maybe nothing. But every day, organizations use data no more substantial than these to make major changes in direction.

It can appear so reasonable: A + B = C. But are D through Z a reality that we don't even comprehend? Why *are* our customers leaving us? What *does* keep our noncustomers from joining us? Where is all of the key information that we *don't* know? Shouldn't we investigate before we invest?

This problem of building big conclusions out of little facts can be overcome only by a passion for understanding that exceeds our rational need to draw conclusions.

Rational processes like traditional strategic planning, with their ritualistic time frames, work against this passion for understanding. We haven't thought things through, but we have to formulate a program and put something into the budget. In a huge irony, the rational process becomes the enemy of reason—the sacred process allows no time or resources to think the problem or opportunity all the way through.

The passion for understanding is a passion to be right rather than an effort to be reasonable. As they say on *The X Files*, "The truth is out there." To find it, it is always safer—and usually more interesting—to assume that we just don't know.

The Narrowness of Education and Experience

The potential hazards of drawing conclusions from insufficient data are greatly increased when our lack of knowledge extends beyond the details of a given situation to a more general ignorance about the world.

We often see this happen when someone rises out of a specialty (e.g., Finance, Marketing, Operations) to the rank of CEO. Limitations come from several directions. Problems and opportunities can be viewed through the grid of the specialty. A financial perspective might lead to too much caution, while a marketing perspective might lead to too much risk.

But perhaps even more devastating is the CEO's absence of knowledge about other critical areas. There is no cheap or easy way to overcome this deficit. The need is not for exposure, but rather for *immersion*. Exposure is useful and can broaden our view, but only immersion can truly conquer narrowness.

Marketing and sales groups fail all the time on precisely this issue of narrowness. They assume that what customers are currently buying is "solid" and "gospel," and reflexively project these "trends" into the future. They too easily reject new ideas, claiming that "nobody is buying that," "no one else is doing that," and "there's no way anyone will go for that." They want to be fast followers (tailgating the successful) or to be on the cutting edge without taking any risks (not possible in the existing universe). And if the new idea has even a slight resemblance to an earlier idea that failed, they all too readily assign the new idea to the ash heap.

It isn't "reasonable" that ideas from outside our professions, areas of expertise, or industry should affect us, but it happens all the time. These outside ideas may be, in fact, the most significant catalysts of change. "The changes that affect a body of knowledge most profoundly do not, as a rule, come out of its own domain."[4] It is often the places where the tectonic plates of knowledge abut and overlap that produce the greatest sparks.

What this means in practice is that we have to avoid hiring and promoting narrow, rational specialists. To be sure, everyone needs to have one or two specialties, areas of expertise that he or she has gained through education and experience. But the very nature of developing an expertise makes it a focused and exclusionary endeavor. Everything that is not part of the specialty has to be pushed aside. In a sense, narrow specialists can learn only more of what they already know, can think about a problem only in the terms they already understand.

We need to encourage "deep generalists," people who have some knowledge and awareness of at least a few areas outside of their specialties. This can be addressed through the variety of outside courses we insist they select from, the inside training that shows marketers how to run a pro forma and production people how a design is conceived, or the kinds of interesting and quaint teams we form and unleash. We can challenge people to challenge themselves. We can create teams that include people who know nothing about the issue or problem at hand.

This leads to an either/or that worries many people. Should we have deeply-trained, expert specialists, or should we have widely trained, questioning generalists? The answer is yes, and more. Yes, we need them—and they need to be the same people. Everyone needs knowledge of a specialty to add value through depth. And everyone needs general knowledge to add value through breadth.

Working "authoritatively" off limited education or experience is like carving out a one-inch hole in the ice on a frozen windshield and concluding that you can see enough to drive safely (you can't—I've tried). Much better decisions are made by taking the time to clear the windshield, to get a full perspective, than by fighting to the death for the little bit that we are squinting to see. We need to encourage a passion for breadth as well as depth.

The Non-Self-Evident Nature of Truth

"If truth were self-evident," said the Roman writer Cicero, "eloquence would not be necessary."

Truth is down there somewhere, but it is not nearly so obvious as it might appear to be.

• Fierce, nasty, command-control managers tell their bosses that they care about their people. Without some kind of 360-degree review, an organizational ombudsman, an anonymous survey, or some other way of circumventing the chain of command (read: control), those further up the management chain are staring at a façade that can hide the devil's own.

• People moan about the loss of employee loyalty (perhaps a starting place to look for what happened would be the notion that people are employees). We might suggest that the root cause lies in the "fact" that people are much less tied to family, community, and church than they used to be, and thus have no framework for loyalty. But this assumption misses the deeper reality that people long to be committed, crave to belong to something valuable, and—especially in a time when other institutions have lost their moral force—need to be committed to something, to anything worthy of their commitment. And we may have a deeper problem. We may hope for loyalty, by which we mean, "You're with us through thick and thin, even if we treat you like dirt," instead of offering mutual commitment to an agreed-upon vision and goal, by which we mean, "You'd be crazy to leave us if we develop you to win, and you'd be crazy to stay if we didn't."

• One of the simplest organizational "truths" is that "what gets measured gets done." But the real truth is that even if we measure the dickens out of things, they still may not get done. We can measure the wrong things. Or we can completely miss a whole bunch of things that need to be measured. The most important measurement in any organization is morale, the level of positive (or negative) passion. How many organizations measure morale?

• The conventional wisdom is that we have to manage people to get results—how can we expect them to perform if we aren't watching them? But no one needs to be managed more, controlled more, or supervised more. Instead, people need to be led more, so that they can effectively manage themselves. Those who can't or won't manage themselves need counseling and, if that fails, should be let go so that they can learn about personal responsibility.

• It would appear that in times of low unemployment and great demand for good people, we need to ease up on our requirements— make the selection process less strenuous, be less demanding, accept marginal people. But this can easily be a self-defeating policy: Poorer employees are capable of doing less work not as well, so we need more poor employees. . . . The counterintuitive response is to raise the bar, make it harder to get in, develop an "elite" or "special" feel, and believe that if we build a passionate organization, they will come. Organizations with rigorous selection processes often have people lined up for miles, while organizations that will take anybody end up with nobody.

There is very little truth that is self-evident, from the universe around us (what revolves around what?) to the universe inside us (is salt really good or really bad for us?). As leaders in organizations, we need to spend a large part of our time digging for truth, asking questions, rattling cages, challenging the obvious.

To revisit Cicero, it is reason that gives us our articulateness, but passion that gives us our eloquence. Reason delivers the content, but passion delivers the context. Reason provides the function, but passion provides the form. In other words, people won't act because they know, but only because they believe. Passion drives us to the core of our individual or organizational being, to ask the worthwhile questions, to get at meaning and not just facts.

The Paradoxical Nature of Reality

For decades, people debated the *quality* versus *productivity* "trade-off": "Do you want it fast, or do you want it right?" The trade-off had even seeped into the popular mind, with the folk wisdom that "you get what you pay for." It isn't logical that we can get something better and cheaper at the same time. But that is reality in many organizations today.

Short-term and *long-term* thinking have likewise been viewed as incompatible. Should we improve this quarter's numbers at the expense of next year's? Or should we invest in next year, and to hell with now? It's not logical that organizations can simultaneously focus on two different time frames. But there are those that do it, developing leaders in every nook and cranny, sinking money into research and development and market analysis, and all the while having another record quarter.

And then there is the argument about *evolutionary* versus *revolutionary* change. Is it *kaizen* or *banzai*? Continuous improvement or leapfrogging? Make it a little better or make it different? Yes. It isn't reasonable, but passionate, great organizations do it all the time. They improve it 10 percent, then 20 percent, then 30 percent, then . . . wow! A whole new process or product. Then they improve it 10 percent . . .

Is it solid *partnership* or fierce *competition*? Should we collaborate with our competitors, or should we whip them? The reality is, we partner so that we can compete more effectively, and as we compete this way, we earn the right to partner with more and stronger organizations.

The deeper reality is the logic of the illogical. Great teachers have always posed these dilemmas and conundrums to their students. Great organizations do the same with their members. We can have a passion for the paradox and the deeper truth that lies hidden in its apparent contradiction.

The Inability of Reason to Correct Its Own Errors

The very construction of a rational analysis or defense can work to prevent the correction of its own errors. This is so for several reasons:

- *Reasoning builds on assumptions.* As we discussed earlier, a faulty assumption will lead to a faulty conclusion. Unfortunately, nothing in the rational process requires us to question our assumptions. If we assume that unions are totally opposed to partnering, we can marshall a lot of data to support our assumption, despite the fact that there are unions that are effectively partnering with their organizations. To say it another way, all analysis is based on values and beliefs. The quality of the analysis is beholden to the quality of the beliefs.

- *Reasoning is normally a linear process,* A to B to C to D. By the time we are working on D, there may be nothing to show us that B is wrong. We may be perfectly right in our conclusion that if B, then C; if C, then D, but how do we reverse the process? What is inherent in an analytical process that helps us, or even allows us, to go back and challenge B? Often, only a disaster. In a recent case, a no doubt well-reasoned policy of Chicago's Ravenswood Hospital required ambulance drivers to deliver patients while emergency-room workers stayed at their posts. When fifteen-year-old Christopher Sarcye was shot by gang members, his friends carried him a hundred yards, to within thirty-five feet of the hospital's doors. Hospital workers stood firm on the policy, and for fifteen precious minutes Christopher lay outside, bleeding and unaided. Police officers finally brought him in, where he died an hour later.[5] The starting point—A—needed to be, "It's the wounded kid, stupid."

- *Reasoning gives a feeling of certainty.* Once we have gone through a "rational analysis," it can be very difficult to backtrack and throw it out. It's hard to admit that we might be wrong when we've done so much work in such an analytical manner. We *know* this to be so; surely any reasonable person would agree with us. If we compound the problem by limiting our reading to books and magazines that support our analysis, we're done for. We may be planting a flag of irrationality on the top of a mountain of rational analysis.

- *Reasoning excludes the "unreasonable".* By its nature, reasoning can look favorably only on history ("I can see how this has worked before") or on logic ("I can see how adding this to that should produce this result"). But there are some things that can be felt but not seen—overnight mail, personal computers, passenger minivans. It was passion, not logic, that created these new services and products. The rationale ("this is why this had to happen") always comes later.

The only corrective is to take reason off the throne and let it serve as advisor to the true royalty—passion, with its insight and imagination and dreams.

Reason's Inability to Be Foolproof

Logical, rational plans get subverted all the time by fools. We can't prove things to a fool—the very term *foolproof* is an oxymoron.

But there are two types of fools. The most plentiful are the fools who hold their opinions regardless of the facts. We can show him the numbers, but he'll still think we're playing games; he can try it ten times and get bad results, but still try it an eleventh time; he can be clearly at fault, but never stop searching for a scapegoat; he can smell the alcohol but deny he has a problem. I used to think that if you showed people the facts, they would change. Maybe. But it's not likely.

The other type of fool is those who persist because they see what others can't see with their facts and analysis. William Seward was a fool because he bought Alaska. A mid-fifties fool named Ray Kroc laid aside a lifetime in sales to buy a nothing hamburger joint owned by the McDonald brothers. Ronald Reagan was a fool who broke with the logic of détente and sought to bury totalitarianism instead.

We can always "prove" that *these* fools are wrong.

And if we do, we lose.

"I never discovered anything with my rational mind," said Albert Einstein in a stunning admission. We have to have a passion to be, and for our people to be, the right kind of fool.

The Unreasonableness of the Hard Thing

Our reason can be overwhelmed by our desire to avoid pain.

As individuals, we may know beyond any doubt that we need to get out of that job, end that relationship, fire that miscreant, change our lifestyle. But change, no matter what benefits it offers, always seems painful in advance and often is painful in practice. Because of this discomfort, we can avoid making decisions and taking action that would be to our benefit—clearly an illogical path.

In other words, we are generally logical unless it hurts.

This all gets magnified in social and organizational settings. We know it's our logical, necessary duty to confront an obnoxious friend or colleague, but we don't want to deal with the pain of confrontation. We allow her to cause great harm to others, and end up resenting her, which is a bad substitute for confronting her. We can see the numbers on a product start to slip, but we tweak the product and spend some more money on marketing rather than starting over. We permit power to be hoarded by a department manager because he's "doing a good job" and "hits his numbers," when the reality is that he is a tough nut and we don't want to lose a top performer. Reason is reasonable, except for the pain.

It's more important that the people around us are willing to face the consequences of reason than that they simply be able to reason. It's better to question soon and often, even if it brings pain, than not at all. "The most important quality in a business person . . . will be not marketing genius or infotech savvy or any other kind of functional knowledge, but rather a character trait—a willingness, even an eagerness, to make large, painful decisions," says business writer Geoffrey Colvin.[6]

To do this—to make difficult personal and organizational choices—requires a whole lot more than reason can provide.

That something more is passion.

Is It Hard or Is It Soft?

We enshrine—and overemphasize the value of—reason even with our language.

Reason-related skills (technical expertise, analytical training) are "hard skills." What do we mean by that? In part, we mean that they are easily described, quantified, and repeated. But often there is more: We mean that they aren't messy, challenging, or debatable. And if we're honest, we often mean even more than that: They are solid, real, valuable, the "meat"—in short, the skills worth spending money on.

And then we tiptoe quietly up to the "soft skills"—the passion-related skills, the emotional, social, and spiritual skills. Communication and conflict resolution? Well, okay. Team dynamics and diplomacy? All right, I guess. Visualization and self-actualization? Come on!

Reasoning skills seem hard, but they are really soft, in part for all of the reasons given in this chapter. These other skills, the so-called soft skills, are really hard, in part because they are more likely to produce success over time, and in part because they are harder to learn, teach, and practice.

In a recent survey of 1,000 U.S. executives, two traits came out by far on top for desirability in a job candidate. "(1) A talent for problem solving . . . do you have the imagination—and the dedication—it takes to worry this thing like a dog with a bone until it works? and (2) conscientiousness . . . will you try to do a good job even when you're having a bad day?"[7] Reason won't fight like a dog with a bone, and reason won't persist to turn a bad day into a good one. But passion will.

Passion is the hard skill.

Conclusion

Reason is grand.
Passion is grander.

Notes

1. Noel M. Tichy, *The Leadership Engine: How Winning Companies Build Leaders at Every Level* (New York: HarperBusiness, 1997), p. 177.
2. Michael Specter, "Falling Birthrates Threaten Societies," *The Kansas City Star,* July 12, 1998.
3. For a full treatment of the damage that these kinds of presuppositions can do to an organization and some proposed cures, see my book *Fatal Illusions: Shredding a Dozen Unrealities That Can Keep Your Organization From Success* (New York: AMACOM, 1997).
4. Peter F. Drucker, *Managing in a Time of Great Change* (New York: Truman Talley Books, 1995), p. 78.
5. As reported in *World,* May 30, 1998, p. 8.
6. Geoffrey Colvin, "The Most Valuable Quality in a Manager," *Fortune,* December 29, 1997, p. 279.
7. As reported in *Fortune,* May 25, 1998, p. 202.

3

The Misleading Comfort of Strategic Planning

Method is much, technique is much, but inspiration is even more.

—Benjamin Nathan Cardozo, *Law and Literature*

Facts, as such, never settled everything. They are working tools only. It is the implications that can be drawn from facts that count, and to evaluate these requires wisdom and judgment that are unrelated to the computer approach to life.

—Clarence B. Randall, *Making Good in Business*

. . . the grand fallacy: that analysis can produce synthesis

—Henry Mintzberg, *The Rise and Fall of Strategic Planning*

Strategic planning offers the greatest of comforts: If we can anticipate the future, we can take action today to prepare ourselves for it.

There are a number of problems with this concept.

First, we can't anticipate the future. At best, we can see snippets and pieces, some things in incomplete fashion, others not at all. Forecasts are no more than extrapolations of the past combined with guesses about the future. "The need to scramble makes a mockery of traditional planning tools such as forecasts by the numbers. . . . Order is a temporary illusion, strategy a moving target," says Rosabeth Moss Kanter.[1]

Second, the decisions and actions that we take today help to mold and determine the future. The future isn't static, some predetermined destiny toward which we are hurtling. The future ten or twenty years from now will be what we, individually and collectively, make it to be. Even events outside of our control—recession, inflation, deflation— are limited in their effect by how we respond to them.

Third, anything we do today to prepare for the future shapes what others do, which shapes what we do, round and round, over and over. We anticipate falling demand for a certain product, so we cut prices or offer rebates. Customers respond by buying more and increasing demand, at least in the short run. We increase our capacity to meet the increased demand, but since the increased demand was generated by our actions and not by any long-term structural change in customer choices, prices fall again as supply outstrips demand. It looks as though our view of the future (i.e., falling prices) was correct, but it was our own actions, caused by our view of the future, that created that very future.

Fourth, we can confuse strategic planning with orderly processes, or simply order. Things seem to be working, to be "clicking," like a car in cruise control on a clear highway. Government bureaucracies can convey this sense of order, as they relish their long-term plans. In the early 1990s, the Asian economy appeared to have predictable rates of growth down to a science, but this was a facade hiding the lack of true free-market passion and productive turmoil. It is the predictable, process-oriented, closed, "who you know" bureaucratic deadness of a Washington, D.C., versus the wild, action-oriented, open, "what you know" colliding passion of a New York City. It is Asian *guanxi* versus fire.

Fifth, it assumes that a rational approach to management based on logic and reason can, if well executed, ensure an organization's vitality and future. As we have seen, however, reason by itself is not sufficient for success in the twenty-first century. Novelist Lord Dunsany reminds us that "Logic, like whisky, loses its beneficial effect when taken in too large quantities." Organizations that rely on the "head" approach of reason will ultimately fail against those that rely on the "heart" approach of passion and emotion. At the deepest level, information is not power and knowledge is not power. Instead, truth, wisdom, and passion are power. And knowledge can become truly powerful when used with wisdom and passion.

As Dilenschneider and others have pointed out, strategic planning is based on the concept that the future can be perceived many moves ahead, as in a game of chess played by a master. The reality has probably always been, and certainly is now and will be in the future, that what lies ahead cannot be perceived clearly—at least not in detail or structure. The world is transactional, like a game of pool or billiards, where we can't plan our next move until the balls have stopped moving from the previous shot. Only passionate people, not experts with thick strategic plans, can react quickly enough.

The fact is that plans, even plans with flexibility and a "Plan B," are still set out clearly for all to see and can't be changed daily or weekly. Passionate people, however, can stop moving in one direction and start moving in another instantly, after assessing the lay of the land.

What Is Strategic Planning?

Strategic planning, like reengineering and total quality management, can mean different things to different people.

In a recent survey of senior managers in fifteen countries, 90 percent of the respondents indicated that they use strategic planning. Of those who used it, 28 percent were "extremely satisfied," while 8 percent were "dissatisfied."[2]

But what are we really talking about? Are we all talking about the same thing? It's a bit like asking if organizations consider people to be their most important asset. Who is going to say no? Who is going to say, "We don't do any strategic planning around here—we just wing it"?

If by strategic planning we mean that we think about who we are and where we are going, and ask ourselves some gut-level questions about our fit with our environment, fine. Better than fine—really, truly terrific. We can't steer a large or growing organization by whims and intuition. If Socrates was right and the unexamined life is not worth living, then the unexamined organization won't keep living.

If, on the other hand, we mean "a formalized procedure to produce an articulated result, in the form of an integrated system of decisions,"[3] we are in trouble. Strategic planning is no longer a way to be creative and innovative and "out of the box"; it is now a way to be in control. It becomes a way to generate capital requests and budgets, not ideas and strategies. We can think we have been contemplating future directions when we have really been crunching numbers and establishing controls.

The first meaning described above is not strategic planning at all, but rather strategic visioning and strategic thinking, "a creative phenomenon that depends more on redrawing lines than respecting them."[4] Strategic planning, in practice, can actually be an impediment to strategic thinking. How can people think beyond clearly-articulated, detailed and monitored plans?

Strategic Planning As the Impossible Dream

So we've got to have strategy and we've got to have planning.

But can we have our strategy and plan it, too?

Another definition of strategy is "the science and art of conducting a military campaign in its large-scale and long-term aspects." A plan is "a formulated scheme setting out stages of procedure."

Strategic planning assumes that the two can be combined, in much the same way that military strategists make what they call plans. But what the strategists really do is more akin to Royal Dutch Shell's "Scenario Planning," although even that isn't general or vague enough.[5] The allied invasion of Europe on June 6, 1944, was one of the most planned military invasions in history. But its planners, who had envisioned scenario after scenario, watched many of their projections disappear in the reality of warfare, such as the chaos at Omaha Beach that voided all plans and the fact that some of Germany's best troops weren't even sent into the battle.

War at its core, in its movements and effects and results, is unplanned—much like the free market. The market voided the value of Ford's planning for the Edsel in the 1950s, Detroit's planning for big cars in the early 1970s, and Detroit's planning for small cars in the 1990s.

The problem with trying to combine strategy and planning is that they are two disparate processes. Strategy is primarily concerned with *synthesis*: pulling together dissimilar pieces into a new and meaningful whole. Planning is primarily concerned with *analysis*: pulling apart connected pieces into understandable components. The two approaches are moving in entirely different directions. Strategy is integration and synergy, planning is differentiation and deconstruction. As Mintzberg describes the attempts to mix this organizational oil and water: "The key, if implicit, assumption underlying strategic planning is that *analysis* will produce *synthesis*: decomposition of the process of strategy making into a series of articulated steps, each to be carried out as specified in sequence, will produce integrated strategies. . . . [But] organizational strategies cannot be created by the logic used to assemble automobiles."[6]

Early in my career, I was the manager of planning for Black & Veatch, one of the largest engineering design and construction firms in the world. We were involved with some projects, such as electric-generating stations, that cost $1 billion and took years from conception to startup. We planned in considerable detail the work that hundreds of people would do, always with the goal of completing the project by a predefined start-up date, none of which we ever missed.

But none of this planning had any bearing on whether the project was the right project to build, or whether it was the right use of vast resources. It had no relevance to the question of whether the timing was correct, or whether this was the right kind of plant (gas, coal, nuclear). These strategic questions had to be answered by some other means. In a sense, all we could do was plan what others had already strategized.

Planning is a good concept when it is applied to specific tasks and known end points. With its orientation toward breaking down, bringing into focus, and organizing details, it's the typical method used to create budgets or outline programs. But planning fails miserably when it is laid on top of a multifaceted present heading toward an infinitely variable future. When we lay the scientific approach of planning onto a largely artistic strategizing about the future, we have bred a donkey with a horse and ended up with a mule. It can't breed anything new, and it's harder than hell to move.

In addition, there is that nasty intruder called reality that alters strategies and can, as a result, demolish plans. I was the project manager on a huge fuel-grade ethanol plant at a time when petroleum prices were high and future resource availability was cloudy. It was a beautiful, renewable, multipurpose concept: Turn corn into high-octane ethanol and produce DDGS, a high-grade animal feed with better nutrients than were in the corn with which we started. The project was, incredibly, driven by a coalition of over a thousand large farmers. And then the oil/gasoline picture changed. The project was noble, but it disappeared.

The point is not that planning is bad or wrong, but rather that planning is not enough at best and the wrong tool at worst. It is necessary, but not sufficient or primary. It has always been limited as a tool and deceptive in its apparent authority. It is a long way around and a long way down the wrong road to take the differential calculus of planning and turn it wondrously into the integral calculus of strategy.

Strategic planning teaches that proper documentation and modeling will produce accurate and usable forecasts of the future, but it promises much more than it can ever deliver. It may, in fact, deliver the opposite: a way to cripple the future. Strategic planning will not help us get a strategy (it will merely operationalize our strategy), but it may prevent a new strategy from being created or developed (by incrementalizing current strategies and extrapolating the status quo).

"Rather than continue to provide a map to a possible future, the plan too often becomes a static entity, rigid, resistant to change, an end in itself. When new ideas erupt from the non-static world beyond the corporation, most will sacrifice the ideas for the sanctity of the plan, since it is considered weak if it has to change."[7] I saw this with a client who had already committed nearly $100 million to an expansion project at a business unit whose market had sagged, while another business unit in a profitable and growing market was starved for capital. It's the plan as king rather than the plan as servant.

Strategy As Organizational Process Rather Than Planning Process

The purpose of strategy is to take our organization effectively into a better future state. There is no question that this is a crucial process.

But this doesn't tell us what the process should look like. Should it be done by the few or the many? Infrequently or continuously? In the planning department or in the trenches?

The goal is to get *everyone* involved in this critical futuristic activity. "If you've got a couple of people sitting in some room trying to dream up [what today's customer might need or want] versus a whole organization who is working at trying to dream that up . . . just think of how much more of an impact you're going to have," Roy Coleman, director of manufacturing projects for Harley-Davidson Motor Company, told me. "When you've got an organization that is thinking that way, rather than just a strategic planning group that is thinking and planning that way, it is just much more powerful." We need everyone in our organization to think strategically, not just a few planning gurus at the top. If the opposition has ten strategic planners and we have a thousand people thinking strategically, we will win.

We need to take it even further. We need everyone thinking this way *all the time*. It has to be built into the process. We can't afford an annual planning ritual with published results that can't be revised or scrapped for another quarter or year. Continuous discussion has to become the foundation for continuous improvement and continuous success. "In the emerging knowledge economy, it's not the organization with the ever-elusive, monolithic 'best plan' that wins, but rather the one with the best minds perpetually collaborating."[8]

And strategy has to be done "out there," in the trenches. After all, everybody has the power to either implement or block the strategy, so why not get their buy-in by including them in the process? In fact, buy-in becomes much less of an ordeal, and perhaps close to automatic, when everyone is already involved. The reality in most organizations is quite the opposite—or worse. In many organizations, most people don't even *understand* the strategy. In a survey of human resource executives attending the Conference Board's 1998 HR conference, "only five percent said all their employees understood their company's business strategy." Fifty-eight percent said "only some" or "few" employees understood.[9] This is pathetic to say the least.

Involvement means that everyone has to have access to virtually all information in a "no hidden agenda" environment. "The only information we don't share is disciplinary action," Karl Eberle, vice president and general manager of Harley-Davidson's Kansas City plant, told me. "Now, some of it we have to be careful how we frame so we don't have any implications on the stock market. But generally we are very, very open. More than most people would ever dream. I err on the side of overcommunication." It has been said that all of our people (assuming we've done a decent job of hiring) will come to the same conclusions as top management if they are given the same information. But it may even be better than that: They might come to some different conclusions.

And some of them could be even better.

Strategic Vision and Strategic Thinking

Strategy is a good concept when it is applied, not to planning, but to directions and the future. It implies that we take the best of what we have learned from the past and the best of what we truly know in the present, and combine this information with our feel for where the future is going *and where we want it to go*. It's an outline, a mix of science and art. When applied correctly, it gives us our organizational vision.

Strategic vision is the first and perhaps most critical advantage of any organization. Who are we, and who do we want to become? What is our reason for existence? Do we have a cause worth fighting for?

Strategic thinking answers basic questions about ourselves and our environment. What are our strengths, our core competencies, our talents—what do we do better than anyone else? And does anyone out there care? Does the marketplace value our strengths, and if so, how and how much?

On the other side, what are our weaknesses and vulnerabilities? Are any of them potentially fatal? How do we eliminate activities that play to our weaknesses, or strengthen those that we simply cannot eliminate? What organizations out there will be able to exploit our weaknesses? What developing trends—especially from groups outside our industry—have the potential to wipe out our market or wipe out us?

Strategic thinking drives us to ask ourselves what we will have to be good at in the future, whereas strategic planning drives us to ask ourselves what we will have to do to optimize current operations. At the center of all of this should be *passion*. Does our vision excite us? If the answer is "no," or if we are "unsure," we need to find and articulate a vision because right now we don't have one (we'll discuss how to develop a vision in Chapter 13).

Are we excited about our strengths and opportunities? If not, we need to toss them overboard and develop some strengths and find some opportunities that we can be fired up about. Ultimately, our passion about our ideas and capabilities should be the fundamental driver of our strategy. Perhaps core competencies aren't as important as core passions.

Some questions to guide our strategic thinking are listed below. Unless our strategic planning process can answer questions like these, it is ultimately worthless to our organization and our people.

Strategic Thinking Questions

1. What is your greatest passion for our organization?
2. What would need to change to see that desire fulfilled?
3. When you think of our organization, the first word that comes to mind is _____.
4. Describe our organization in 25 words or less.

5. What do we do better than anyone else? How passionate are you about this? How do we maximize this competency?
6. What are we doing that we need to outsource or stop doing? How do we drop it? Will this leave us vulnerable to our competitors?
7. What is the most important thing we should/could be doing today to lead us into a successful future?
8. What could we do to build trust and commitment in our people? What obstacles are preventing this?
9. What is the top way our organization could better and more passionately serve its stakeholders?
10. If a major magazine wrote an article on our organization in ten years, how would the headline read?

Strategic vision and thinking involve *sight*. "Strategic thinking has two major components: Insight about the present and foresight about the future."[10] They differ from strategic planning in that they offer, not a predetermined plan for the future, but a vision of who we are and who we want to become. They encourage us to get outside of daily reality and presuppositions and logical extrapolations to accurately fit and mold our organization into the future.

But there is one more critical component of strategic vision and thinking. *If* people really are our most important asset, and *if* the global economy really is moving from an industrial/capital base to a knowledge base, and *if* the only thing that will make us different (and hopefully better) in five years is the passion and ideas of our people, we will need to make commitment to our own people the core of our strategy.

"The strategies that get implemented most effectively," says Arthur Wainwright, chairman and CEO of Baldrige Award winner Wainwright Industries, "are those that make the protection and development of people the overriding consideration in every decision that is made. . . . Our planning process is driven first and foremost by our commitment to people—not only because it produces better bottom-line results, but because it's the right thing to do."[11]

Strategic vision can no longer be the work of the lone visionary who visualizes what the organizational machine should look like five years down the road. It has to be an organically produced, widely held view of the pulsing organism we must become if we are to thrive in that future environment. It has to be a synthesis and extension of all that we are and possibly can be.

A Different Kind of Planning

To be effective in this world of the future, we will need at least three kinds of planners:

1. *Deliberate.* These are the people who take the conclusions reached by strategic visioning and thinking and convert them into realistic goals for the short- and long-term future. Serious, focused, analytical people belong here. They need to be able to convert the big picture into operational and financial targets, and to evaluate available resources and whether current systems and structures can effectively utilize them. Their focus is on current core competencies.

2. *Emergent.* These are the people who cull from a passionate organization the ideas and suggestions that the synthesizers can use to create whole new strategies or modify existing ones. Enthusiastic, expansive, sociable people belong here. They need to be able to listen to ideas, monitor trends, and ensure that the tacit knowledge and untacit passion in the organization is heard. Their focus is on new, possible, hinted-at core competencies, including those that may not be in current organizational favor, and they nurture them and work hard to keep them alive.

3. *Synthesizing.* These are the people who pull all of the deliberate and emergent components together in an ebbing and flowing mass of constantly evolving and revising strategy. These are probably the true strategists, and they should probably be called that rather than planners. Wild, imaginative, paradoxical people belong here. If they don't make us feel uncomfortable, we've got the wrong people. These are the people who help the organization see how to close the gaps between our strategic vision and thinking on the one hand, and our current operational reality on the other.

These planners and strategists are only facilitators and catalysts of an organizationwide focus on strategy. Strategy is everyone's domain. But without a structure to support it and proper mechanisms to ensure that it happens, the vibrancy of passionate, synthesizing strategizing will collapse into the dead, fixed-point world of strategic planning.

Strategizing needs to shift from an annual event with monitoring to an ongoing process that monitors itself. At Coca-Cola, for example, "Business planning is no longer an annual ritual but a continual discussion."[12] At Wainwright Industries, strategy leaders meet weekly to discuss where they are and where they want to go.

Strategy is life. "Visualize strategy not as a formal set of documents, but as a dynamic decision-making process . . . a perpetual stream of focused conversations to develop an exciting, coherent, ever-evolving 'motion picture' of the organization."[13]

Strategizing—giving a forum to strategic vision and strategic thinking—is the heart of future success. Just as with people, the heart has to beat all of the time.

Conclusion

Strategy, in many organizations, has no soft side.

Nuances give way to numbers. Possibilities are made to yield to processes. And dreams fade under the relentless flow of details. We can't step back and think because we've got too much planning to do. We dissect but we don't connect. Strategy has far too many people with scissors and far too few with tape.

War is too important to be left to the generals, and strategy is too important to be left to the analysts.

In the end, strategy and planning can have a decent friendship—but they make a truly awful marriage.

Notes

1. Rosabeth Moss Kanter, *On the Frontiers of Management* (Boston: Harvard Business School Press, 1997), p. 61.
2. As reported in *Fortune*, September 7, 1998, p. 163.
3. As defined by Henry Mintzberg, *The Rise and Fall of Strategic Planning* (New York: The Free Press, 1994), pp. 12 and 31.
4. Mintzberg, p. 77.
5. Scenario planning is laying out a number of different future paths or states, and then asking what could or should be done to prepare for each of them. It's a way of taking the sting out of the future by thinking about it in detail in the present.

For a good discussion of scenario planning, see Gill Ringland, *Scenario Planning: Managing for the Future* (New York: John Wiley & Sons, Inc., 1998).

6. Mintzberg, p. 13.
7. Jerry Hirshberg, *The Creative Priority* (New York: HarperBusiness, 1998), p. 219.
8. Oren Harari, "Attracting the Best Minds," *Management Review*, April 1998, p. 23.
9. As reported in the BNA *Bulletin to Management*, November 12, 1998, p. 355.
10. T. Irene Sanders, *Strategic Thinking and the New Science: Planning in the Midst of Chaos, Complexity, and Change* (New York: The Free Press, 1998), p. 10.
11. Arthur D. Wainwright, "People Must Be the Central Core of the Strategic Planning Process," *Strategy & Leadership*, reprint of January/February 1997 article.
12. Betsy Morris, "Doug Is It," *Fortune*, May 25, 1998, p. 74.
13. Oren Harari, "Catapult Your Strategy over Conventional Wisdom," *Management Review*, October 1997, p. 24.

4

The Siren Song of the Learning Organization

By annihilating the desires, you annihilate the mind. Every man without passions has within him no principle of action, nor motive to act.

—Claude Adrien, *Helvetius*

Those who judge by their feelings do not understand reasoning, for they wish to get an insight into a matter at a glance, and are not accustomed to look for principles. Contrarily, others, who are accustomed to argue from principles, do not understand the things of the heart, seeking for principles and not being able to see at a glance.

—Blaise Pascal, *Pensees*

It is a capital mistake to theorize before one has data.

—Arthur Conan Doyle

The concept of the learning organization is valuable, and certainly a major part of the success equation. But it isn't the magic pill.

And it isn't enough.

What Is Learning?

At first glance, learning appears to be the acquisition of new knowledge and skills: I don't know anything about this; I am given or find or lay out a course of study; I absorb the information; I apply it if appropriate.

A to B to C to D. Once again, reason gives us the linear approach. Our education has a "strategic plan." If we're not careful, we can lose the big picture and the synthesis altogether as we divide and conquer the knowledge.

But learning is much more than this.

Real learning is about *changing* and *becoming*. Every time we learn something new, we have a choice: We can accept it or reject it, implement it or let it atrophy, synthesize it with the rest of our knowledge grid or let it lie there, isolated.

It is too easy to reject knowledge or let it atrophy or let it lie there. This is why most "learning" is really just accumulation of information. One definition of a typical college lecture is: "Information passing from the notes of the teacher to the notes of the student without going through the mind of either one." ("I never let my schooling interfere with my education," said North American writer Mark Twain.)

This is also why many "learning organizations" are really training organizations (think of seals) and not learning organizations at all. We are in trouble when we use the terms *learning* and *training* interchangeably. I can learn how to train my dog, but I can't be trained to teach my dog how to learn.

Learning is a *whole* lot harder than training.

The Components of Learning

What are some of the components of learning? What makes learning different from training?

• Learning requires more than technical skills (listening, note taking). It requires whole-being openness to new thoughts.

• Learning involves the destruction of old grids, existing connections, reflexive responses. Learning is a subversive activity.

• Learning demands an intimate involvement with the topic at hand and everything it relates to. There is neutral training, but there is no neutral learning.

• Learning needs dialogue. There have to be questions and feedback and correction, then more questions. We can't seek closure too soon, or "theorize before all the data is in."

- Learning has to encourage creative assembly. How does this information fit with what we already know? Does it tell us that some of what we "know" just ain't so? How might it tie in with everything else we are learning?

- Learning has to be expansive. Broader is better. What can "The Charge of the Light Brigade" teach us about organizational loyalty—and lunacy? What does the loss of territory in the Western Hemisphere, first by Spain and then by Mexico, teach us about overextension and fierce competition from late arrivals? Does the replacement of mainframes by personal computers tell us anything about how we should organize our people?

- Most of all, learning requires passion. *We remember and use little or nothing of that which doesn't stir us.* Smart, determined people can learn things about which they are not passionate, but only if they are passionate about what the acquired knowledge will permit them to do.

True learning is a force, not a program. Many so-called "learning organizations" are really programmatic training organizations with the wrong name. We can develop a learning organization, an organization that shares the components above. But we will have a very difficult time trying to organize learning. It can't be formulated, and it won't be bottled.

Why Should We Learn?

Many people today would agree that we need to learn continuously. Lifelong learning has become an accepted part of both work and personal philosophy. The idea of learning for sixteen or more years followed by a forty-year implementation phase has become not only unworkable but absurd. In truth, turning on our minds in our youth and then turning them off forever was always a pretty poor way to live. Retirement as a "do-nothing" time of life is just the logical extension of this numbing "learn–do–rest," approach to nonliving.

Why do we need to learn continuously?

- *Because every sane and reasonable human being is a living, dynamic organism that has an orientation toward growth.* We need to grow to fulfill our raison d'être. Experience teaches that after they reach middle age, most people grow only in their physical dimensions. However, some never stop growing in the important ways.

• *Because we don't want to be pathetic, raging against the new and demanding that our lives be kept the same, willing to fight to the death for the status quo.* I wrote my first book in longhand and went through torturous edits with revisions typed on a typewriter. Was there any glory in that? Bring on the newest software! Change is a component of success, change is good, change is exciting, change is *life*; in fact, our excellent response to, and initiation of, change will be one of our sustainable competitive advantages. The world has many problems, yes; perhaps we can help solve them. And the world has many opportunities, yes; perhaps we can make them ours.

• *Because we will achieve little, if anything, without it.* In a knowledge economy, we will have to "earn" and "save" more and more knowledge if we want to be "knowledgeably independent." We can be more in the future than we are today. There is always another opportunity, always a second chance.

• *Because any useful learning on virtually any topic will enrich our work and personal lives in ways that, at times, will astonish us.* This is especially so when what we are learning in a number of different areas coalesces into something wonderfully brand new, and we discover new ways to solve our problems or satisfy our yearnings. Looking at many different perspectives on the same topic can also open our eyes. Without reading them right away, I save magazine articles by major topics; then I read them as a set. It is totally amazing how many insights flow out of the interconnections of so many perspectives.

• *Because it will enable us to become wise and not just old.* We need to learn to become better people so that we can make a difference in our world, rather than expending our time and energy just moving up the ladder or making more money. Our names may be forgotten after we die, but the imprint of our values and contribution will work its way through future generations as surely as our genetic makeup—and perhaps with more effect.

We have to search the reasons given above and our own hearts and minds to find and embrace a reason to learn that is deeper and more compelling than simply the accumulation of knowledge (or worse, information). Without this reason, we're likely to find that our time and energy are too precious to expend on the tough task of learning, and the knowledge that we do attain will be limited at best, and worthless or even damaging at worst. (For example, because it is incomplete or too narrow in perspective.)

The proverb tells us that "knowledge puffs up." That is, knowledge, by itself and without a proper use, can easily lead to pomposity and arrogance. The modern tendency to be enraptured with credentials and jargon shows where this can lead. We confuse knowledge with wisdom, which is knowledge that is properly applied.

In order to become wise, we need to have the drive to learn and the insight to use what we learn, but also the humility to know how little we know and the curiosity to learn more.

Why Don't We Learn?

Since learning is so important, why don't we do it? What is the missing piece?

Passion. Passion drives what we do, and even determines what we perceive. We perceive and think about only what we care about. We can scan newspapers and magazines and never take notice of a certain problem, injury, or sickness—until the moment that we experience it. Then it leaps off the page. We feel the "hurt," share the experience, hope for some sense of victory. Likewise, we can be the smartest work group in the world, but if we aren't really passionate about what we're doing, a lot of our creativity and many of our ideas are going to stay locked up in our heads. "You can have all the intelligence in the world, but if you don't have that desire or that passion to really, truly make it the very best, you will never be the very best," Roy Coleman of Harley Davidson told me.

One leader from a company with which I was consulting told me about a benchmarking team from his organization that had visited his former employer. The team members had come back quite enthusiastic about a unique practice that was benefiting the company they had visited, and that they were sure would benefit their organization as well. The irony of their proposal was that this leader had been the driving force behind getting his former employer to adopt this practice. He had been trying for quite some time to introduce it at his current company, but no one would listen. They couldn't "hear" it until they had seen it in action and were passionate about what it could do.

Of course, we need to gather information and process it. But there is more: In order to capitalize on and exploit changes in the world around us, we need to be passionate about learning, about teaching, about growth, about change, about being flexible and adaptable, about the future, about our role in that future, and about abandoning what we have already learned when it loses validity or no longer works for us.

Learning organization theory says that the root of our weaknesses, failings, and problems is ignorance. The passionate organization knows that there is a deeper cause: lack of passion. Passion, not the dispensing of knowledge, must be the starting point if real learning is to occur.

It is the absence of passion, or not making passion the starting point, that hinders the effectiveness of learning organizations.

How Will We As Individuals Learn?

First, we have to know what we want to learn. This has both short- and long-term implications. In the short term, it means that we ask two questions: What do I need to know to do the work at hand better? and, What do I have a passion to learn about, whether or not I can see its immediate application? The answers to these questions will at times coincide and at times not. If they never come together, it means that we are very badly mismatched to our work.

In the long term, we have to evaluate what we want our core competencies to be in the next five to ten years. Asking what our core competencies are today is a useful question, *but only as a starting point*. Where we are today will be meaningless and useless in a very short time. We learn and grow or we shrivel and die. There is no neutral, no idle, no holding action.

Once we've determined what we want our core competencies to be, we can measure that goal against where we are right now. Some future competencies can be built on what we are already good at, while others will need whole new embarkations. Some current competencies will have to be abandoned. And we'll have to be careful not to build on, or even spend much time trying to improve, our weaknesses. This is especially important if we don't like those areas (which is probably why they are weaknesses in the first place). The only exceptions are areas of weakness (like communication skills) that could undermine our success.

Then we can develop a plan to get from where we are to where we want to be. We can ask our organization to help us, but ultimately it's ours to win or lose. I remember the first time I paid my own money to attend a seminar that the organization I worked for might or might not have approved. It was a liberating experience that would have been cheap at twice the price.

Second, we have to make sure that we have looked at all of the possible sources from which we can learn—all of the possible teachers under whom we can study. It is too easy, for example, to turn to a course on psychology or sociology or to a seminar on team building for answers to the question of how people can best work together. It is much more expansive and can be very useful to see what history (e.g., Stephen Ambrose's review of the Lewis and Clark expedition), biographies (e.g., Martin Gilbert's life of Winston Churchill), and novels (e.g., Ernest Hemingway's *For Whom the Bell Tolls*) might teach us on the subject.

"Every day, I have to make difficult decisions, and I base them primarily on what has happened in the past," says Nathan Myhrvold, chief technology officer of Microsoft Corporation. "History can lead you to see important abstractions, and it also offers great lessons. . . . If you want to make good decisions about what's to come, look behind you."[1] We have to look backward to move forward. We need to develop a passion for history, including the history of our own lives, our organization, and our industry.

Third, we have to see the difference between continuous and discontinuous learning. Continuous learning, making every assignment or project a learning experience, is a very useful way of life, and may possibly even be a lifesaver. But if we're not careful, it can also be a giant obstacle to out-of-the-box, discontinuous thinking—reframing, rethinking, reimagining who we are and what we want to become. The continuous learning and improvement philosophy of *kaizen* is valuable but also "is seductive because it whispers to us that we don't have to reinvent today's products and today's way of managing our enterprises; instead, we can adjust and improve and make the status quo better. . . . This sort of *kaizen* mind-set engenders a false sense of security."[2] We can't afford to let our learning get into such a steady flow that we miss the discontinuities, the ambiguous things that can't be structured into a training book or workshop.

Effective leaders in the coming years will ask some serious questions of those whom they are leading: Where do you want to be? Does this align with where we need you to be? Do we even know what that is? Where can we help you? Where can you help yourself? What is the available array of knowledge? How can we help you know what's in the box, and when to get out of it as well?

Once we are asking these questions of ourselves and each other, continually and sincerely, we have the makings of a true learning organization.

The True Learning Organization

A true learning organization begins with an attitude.

It's an attitude that says that almost all people are capable of doubling their knowledge and tripling their wisdom—all they need is the passion and the resources. This suggests that the organization can be structured (or destructured) in such a way that learning will be enhanced rather than stripped down, shared rather than hoarded.

A true learning organization encourages people, individually and in groups, to gather information, explore ideas, evaluate past performance and future needs, challenge assumptions, give and receive feedback, and share what is learned. It is an open system, with free and nurtured access and an unchartable number of linkages.

And it has some mechanisms—not policies, procedures, systems, or processes, but some facilitating *mechanisms*—to ensure that the learning stays free and open, just a bit on the wild side, and far from traditional training.

It can be fed, but not led or controlled, by an organizational learning center or "university." It can include individual, customized career development plans. It can incorporate tools to make knowledge transparent, from a simple organizational "yellow pages" of subject matter experts to a full-blown "knowledge network" (with entry determined by passion for the topic as well as by experience).

In a sense, not only is a true learning organization far beyond a traditional program of structured training, it is far beyond what many people think when they hear the term *learning organization*. In reality, it is a *developing* organization—developing individuals, interrelationships, teams, skills, knowledge, wisdom, theory, and application.

But the key question is: Is it alive? You can walk past two school classrooms, both at the same grade level, and tell within seconds which one is a learning organization and which one is a learning graveyard.

A true learning organization is an incredible competitive advantage. And to build on the passion of our people and have its greatest impact, it also has to be a teaching organization.

The Teaching Organization

A learner can't learn unless there are teachers. A learning organization can't learn unless it is also a teaching organization. But most organizations are even less geared toward teaching than they are toward learning.

What do we mean? People are not required to share what they learn. Learning (training) is considered an expense rather than an investment. Mechanisms to transfer knowledge effectively and consistently are not established. Nobody knows whom to ask in order to avoid reinventing solutions that have already worked elsewhere in the organization, or to avoid attempting solutions that have already failed.

To teach is to learn. Nothing drives learning more than having to teach it. In order for an organization to become a teaching organization, it already has to be a learning organization. But just as people need a reason to learn, so they need a reason to teach. In one *Fortune* 1000 company, when we surveyed all employees and asked, "What assets are we currently underutilizing?" the top two answers were "the knowledge and experience of all employees" and "the creativity and ideas of all employees." They had the stuff to teach, but they weren't teaching. The number of new ideas and the amount of transferred knowledge were pitifully small. Everyone had—and most were using—the power to do nothing.

Why would our people want to teach?

• Because we have abandoned top-down management and have chosen to give more than lip service to developing leaders at every level.

• Because they believe that what they know is valued by the organization and will be valuable to the learners. This means that we have to find ways to show them that we value their knowledge and creativity, by honoring and publicly recognizing their teaching efforts and, where appropriate, rewarding them as well. Professional groups and societies have known this for a long time—people share everything they are learning primarily to receive the accolades of their peers.

• Because we have emphasized consistently the importance of learning, and so there is a ready-made and willing audience for the teaching.

• Because we have put teaching on an equal footing with learning. We treat teaching and learning as equals, in terms of resources allocated and recognition given.

• Because we have created forums where teachers can be true mentors and leave a legacy behind them. From sponsors assigned at orientation and during the probation (read: learn a lot) phase, through rotating team leadership positions, to intranet "learning exchanges" and experience-filled "yellow pages," we can make sure that the people who have already learned can teach those who need to.

• Because we are willing to spend the money to make teaching, and thus learning, a reality.

• Because everyone is evaluated on (1) what they are learning and (2) how many people they have taught it to. At Saturn, leaders are required to teach; they are given credit for their own development when they teach others.

Threats to the Passionate Organization's Ability to Learn

Being passionate about learning and teaching is different from simply emphasizing their importance. The structures can all be in place but be lifeless, like a body without blood.

Too many organizations, as soon as they discover learning, want to organize it, systemize it, measure it, replicate it. They fall into the reason trap all over again. If we can just get learning down to . . . well, a *science*. If we could just do that, we could embrace the beautiful siren who is singing to us, telling us to come near.

But we will crash on the rocks. True learning—and certainly passion, for learning or anything else—will not flourish in this half-training, half-proceduralized, bogus learning organization, in which we make a microscopic effort to make sure all of the "learning pieces" are in place and that everyone "gets trained."

Often, the problem is too narrow a view of learning. We too easily associate learning with the left-brained, analytical, logical, hard skills. Math, verbal, and technical skills become paramount. This stuff is easy to process, easy to test, and easy to verify. Unfortunately, it is only one piece of the learning puzzle.

What about the other aspects of learning? What about the right-brained, creative, associative pieces? Interpersonal issues, dealing with ambiguity, deeper levels of problem solving, or creativity may be harder to learn and verify, but may be even more critical to our organization's success.

It's not that these are always more important than the analytical variety; they're just easier to ignore and give short shrift to. This tacit, emerging knowledge is subtle, fragile, and intermingled, and not just linear and obvious. It's the stuff in the gaps, the cracks, the haze, the fog. It's the life-saving idea that is still so tiny that it can be destroyed easily before it reaches its full power, as though an Augustine, a Shakespeare, a Newton, or a Dostoevsky was snuffed out as an infant.

Other factors can also convert the passionate organization into the training organization or even the crippled organization. Some of these include:

- We've gone through a process of renewal and have started doing some things in a new way. Now this new approach has been written into corporate lore and has become "the way." But when the market and the rest of our environment changes, will "the way" still work?
- We've gone through a process that is supposed to make us a high quality organization—benchmarking, ISO certification, one of the many quality awards. Now we somehow, maybe even unintentionally, have concluded that we've arrived. If we aren't careful, these processes can cause as many problems as they solve, or even more. Best practices are changing all of the time; at any one point in time they are only approximations of reality.
- We've codified what we believe to be the best ways into all sorts of organizational documents: policy manuals, procedural manuals, executive memos, and job descriptions. People keep messing up (sometimes erroneously trying another way,

sometimes reasonably trying another way), so we keep trying to close the loopholes with more documents and amendments. There is no "one best way."

- We've started trying to measure and control "intellectual capital" the way we do plant, equipment, production, and revenues. But plants don't have brilliant insights, equipment doesn't give two weeks' notice, production doesn't reinvent itself, and revenues don't have bad moods. The very act of measurement tends to label, categorize, and limit; and our very involvement in measurement, as scientists are aware, can change what we are measuring. We need to measure, but more loosely.

Learning that is codified, stratified, and rigidified is no longer learning at all. We have reached the dangerous moment in the life of a learning/teaching organization when our "learning" and "teaching" begin to annihilate our passions, our desires, and our creativity.

When our feeble, best shots at reality *become* our reality, we have stopped being a true learning or teaching organization. Our learning is now about how to follow the rules, and our teaching is the rote instruction of the harsh old schoolmaster.

Protecting the Passionate Organization's Ability to Learn

How do we assure that the passionate organization doesn't become rigidified?

First of all, we cannot afford to have our learning/teaching organization run only by analytical types. This kind of education/training looks neat and tidy, and it is neat and tidy. It's just not enough. To go back to our planning model, we need deliberate educators, who can lay out the rational/logical areas; emergent educators, who can give life to the passionate/emotional/social side; and synthesizing educators, who can interweave them and keep them in balance.

We also must be careful to measure what we can usefully measure without becoming obsessed with measuring. Great ideas often cannot be logically defended in their germinating stages. If they're attacked ("We've never done that before"; "I don't know of anyone else who is doing that"; "Give me a report before you take that any further"), they will almost always die. They have too little form in the early phases, and whatever energy is available has to be spent on forming them if anything useful is to result.

We need to make room for some nonteam players. Teamwork is being oversold (as well as often badly applied), and individual insight and action are often undersold. There are evil people who will destroy our organization if we give them a chance, and there are positive but nonconforming people who will shake our organization to the roots if we give them a chance. Quality leadership knows the difference and forces itself to face it. In the average organization, the political hacks and destroyers are allowed to live on, while the caring maverick is driven out.

We have to see the both/and related to sharing information versus keeping it to ourselves. The learning organization holds sharing and cross-pollinating as two of its highest priorities, and rightly so. But effective organizations and teams often thrive (at least for a time) on secrecy, on being the only ones in the know, and on protecting an idea until it is strong enough to face a hostile environment. "Secrecy has long been a passion for great groups. . . . Secrecy serves to [bind] insiders that much closer together."[3] We have to have an organization that is passionate for knowledge in all of its forms and availabilities; we need to know when to pollinate and when to germinate.

In our organizations, we need the creator, the analyzer, and the synthesizer: a designer to imagine, an engineer to break the idea down, and a conceptualizer to pull it all back together. Each person in the triangle needs to be passionate about his or her own area of expertise, passionate about teaching the others about it, passionate about learning about the alien field, and passionate about giving birth together to something that none could give birth to alone.

Conclusion

Strategic planning has yielded naturally to its younger cousin, the learning organization. Where traditional strategic planning teaches that proper documentation and modeling will produce accurate and usable forecasts of the future, much learning organization theory teaches that properly equipped employees and appropriate systems/structures for acquiring knowledge will produce accurate and usable ways to deal with an unforecastable future. Both rely on the head rather than the heart for their impetus.

But a rationally-based and structured learning organization is a true siren song. It promises competitive advantage where there is little or none, because it has deficiencies in both concept and implementation. Only a passion-based, true learning/teaching organization is built solidly enough on the right foundation, because only people remain as a true competitive advantage.

Rational systems can be clever, they can be right, they can even be useful.

But they will never be enough.

Notes

1. As quoted in *Fast Company*, June/July 1998, p. 84.
2. Oren Harari, "Kaizen Is Not Enough," *Management Review*, September 1997, p. 25.
3. Warren Bennis and Patricia Ward Biederman, *Organizing Genius: The Secrets of Creative Collaboration* (Reading, Mass.: Addison-Wesley Publishing Company, Inc., 1997), p. 81.

5

The Uncontrollable Nature of Fire

A man that is ashamed of passions that are natural and reasonable is generally proud of those that are shameful and silly.

— Lady Mary Wortley Montagu

Enthusiasm is the leaping lightning, not to be measured by the horse-power of the understanding.

— Ralph Waldo Emerson, *Letters and Social Aims*

In things pertaining to enthusiasm, no man is sane who does not know how to be insane on proper occasions.

— Henry Ward Beecher, American clergyman and social reformer

Tom Peters and others have been preaching for years about "turning people loose." Why don't most organizations do it?

There are a number of reasons, but one of the most significant is that many of us—perhaps most of us—are leery about emotion and passion and the soft issues. We sense that, once unleashed, people could take us in unthought-of directions (which we want and don't want at the same time). We want controlled passion, an oxymoron, instead of directed passion, a possibility and necessity.

There are other reasons that we resist betting on people's fire:

1. We have the illusion that only a rational plan, understood and accepted throughout the organization, can give us the necessary linear A-to-Z approach to be successful.[1]

2. We're all from Missouri, the "show-me" state—we don't want to commit our support or resources to something unless and until we can see exactly, step by step, where it's going to take us.

3. We fear that unleashing people will be grossly inefficient, as they will run off in unproductive directions or duplicate efforts.

4. Worse, we fear that people might start challenging the status quo, including some of our own pet theories and past decisions (and even worse, we fear that they might even be right about some of their challenges).

5. We're simply too insecure to let go of command. I've seen too many leaders go to seminars and read books and articles about the necessity of leading rather than managing and guiding rather than controlling, claim to agree with the thinking, and then go back to a command-and-control orientation. It isn't a matter of ignorance, of not knowing—in other words, a rational problem. It's our own emotions, our insecurities, our issues—in other words, our negative passions— that keep us doing what we know to be ineffective or even stupid.

6. We don't feel that we can give this kind of authority to act to people who don't really have a stake in the business. The easiest solution, of course, is to give them a stake in the business—not to just make them *feel* like owners, but let them actually *be* owners.

7. We intend to give them free rein "someday" (forgetting that "someday" isn't a day of the week). We end up in a no-man's-land of talking about freedom, even promising freedom, but never really delivering it. The hesitation and procrastination will kill our organization, as Mikhail Gorbachev found out in a grand way as he presided over the disintegration of the Soviet Union. There are few approaches as harmful as exercising control while dabbling with freedom.

8. We misunderstand the centralization versus decentralization argument. We're concerned about being too decentralized, while at the same time we understand the harm that can come from too much centralization. But the reality is that we don't need one or the other, or more of one than the other; we need both, in equal measure. We need decentralization to get the solutions in close proximity to the problems, and we need centralization to ensure that we move in a powerful, united direction. But here's the critical issue that we can too easily miss on centralization: *We need centralization by alignment with vision and values, not centralization by structure.*

Bound by the Chain of Command

It is this centralization by structure that is the killer.

We know we need centralization, but we apply the wrong method—the costlier method, the more complicated method, the strangling method.

We inherit or begin to build an elaborate structure to give us the centralization that we perceive we need. Workers are watched by supervisors watched by managers watched by department managers watched by plant/site managers watched by division managers watched by vice presidents watched by group vice presidents watched by the president watched by the chairperson/board of directors.

All the watching takes a lot of time and energy, but adds little or no value. In fact, it often takes away value. How?

- The salaries and benefits of all these people are a drag on the organization's financial health. Our fear of freedom drives us to financial incoherence.
- A lot of time and effort has to be spent on communication between the watchers and the watchees, up and down the chain of command. More unproductive mistakes are made because of the inevitable communication breakdowns than would ever be made by simply having unwatched doers.
- Meetings—informational, getting everyone "on board"—soak up an untold amount of time. I hear this over and over again in surveys we tabulate and seminars I present.
- The mission of a watchee becomes pleasing the watcher rather than the customer. To say it another way, the fearsome position of the watcher turns him or her into the only important customer. Vast energies are spent on self-protective documentation ("CYA").
- The mission of a watcher, on the other hand, becomes ensuring that the watchee does nothing to embarrass the watcher with the watcher's watcher.
- Creativity gets stifled. The chain is simply too ponderous and idea-unfriendly to allow new thoughts to occur and make it through the obstacle course all the way to the top. Even accurate *information* has a hard time making it all the way to the top. The chain is an amazing truth-filtering mechanism.

In this kind of environment, the worst offense becomes going around the chain (appropriately named) of command. A watchee in some organizations can do almost anything without getting fired or reprimanded, but heaven help her if she goes directly to her watcher's watcher.

It used to be a sin in virtually all organizations to violate the chain of command.

In the world we're living in now, it should be a sin not to.

Tools of the Chain of Command

The chain of command comes with a whole lot of tools that are vast energy drainers. They do their wasteful jobs in a number of ways: First, they take a lot of time to prepare and update; second, they limit and proscribe rather than enhance and free; and third, they require substantial effort to enforce.

What are they?

- Policy manuals—a rational but poor substitute for a compelling vision
- Procedures manuals—a rational but poor substitute for committed people
- Job descriptions—a rational but poor substitute for ownership
- Performance evaluations—a rational but poor substitute for performance agreements
- Permission slips (such as requests or requisitions)—a rational but poor substitute for action
- Reporting—a rational but poor substitute for mutual trust

It isn't that these tools are always inappropriate. In some situations, legal and otherwise, they may be necessary. The problem comes when we begin to *rely* on these things to make our organizations go. Law doesn't bring life. We can have an organization full of these tools and devoid of any passion. People can be in compliance, and our organizations can still shrivel up.

These tools are logical, they can even appear reasonable, but they can be essentially unnecessary. This is so not because people won't abuse the system, but because passion is more than sufficient to obliterate the need to depend on them. Of course, there will always be some people who are rotten and nasty and greedy. But building a rational, controlling structure for the many to contain the perversities of the few is counterproductive. After years of application, it is often irrational and frequently productive—of negative passions.

In many organizations, these tools are equivalent to the instruments of torture used by the Inquisition. We may beat you and mangle you with these devices, but don't be so foolish as to think they might help you to get to the truth or to do your job.

When True Merit and Freedom Come to Organizations

It is hard to believe that the sweep of liberty, democracy, and free markets throughout the globe can forever be resisted inside our organizations. How can what's good for our country and the world be bad for Joe and Sally employee?

Too many organizations are still little monarchies or fiefdoms. Even leaders who have some good desires to "free up" their people can allow little baronies to exist in pockets of the organization. Make no mistake: People in our employ will judge our degree of freedom, *and thus their response to our request for commitment,* by the liberty nurtured or the slavery imposed by the person to whom they report.

"Communities based on merit and passion are rare."[2] But why is this? How many people in a poll would vote against merit and passion? What's the alternative? Pork-barrel and lethargy?

People who are opposed to emphasizing merit are often driven by an uncomfortable feeling that they themselves don't measure up. Top producers, excellent teachers, committed volunteers—in short, those who are passionate about their work—don't normally have a problem with merit (although they may strongly oppose subjective assessments of merit, at which many, including unions, rightly balk). This is the merit that flows from a passion-oriented culture.

In the same way, those who are opposed to passion are often driven by the inner awareness that they don't have any. "A fox, when he cannot reach the grapes, says they are not ripe," said English clergyman and poet George Herbert. These people fear what they don't understand and what they don't possess. And they don't want to see it in others. "Stop being so emotional," they might admonish an excited employee. What they are really saying is, "Stop making me uncomfortable with your passion."

Our organizations will be built or hampered by the degree of freedom we have made available to them. We generally do this by removing rather than adding. We don't need initiatives to enhance freedom as much as we need initiatives to remove obstacles to freedom.

But Passion Is So . . . Unplanned

Passion is unplanned. And inconsistent. And annoying. Just like life and life's challenges, like life's ebbs and flows.

It has to be unplanned to open the doors to new and currently unanticipated futures. "None of this is about squeezing anything at all—it is about tapping an ocean of creativity, passion, and energy."[3] I think most of us would be absolutely stunned if, we could for a moment, see with our own eyes how much latent passion is out there, ready to be tapped.

Passionate, excellent people may appear at times to be denying reality as they press their ideas or programs. But they aren't denying reality. They are denying the *apparent* obstacles that others or the system *perceives* to be reality. As Walt Disney said, "It's kind of fun to do the impossible." What appears to be so very rational and real or impossible may be nothing more than a smokescreen, or may simply represent a superficial understanding of a deeper reality.

We should want new ideas to flow from every quarter and mess up our deliberate ideas. We want the unplanned to mess up the planned. We *need* this to happen. The ideas that grow out of people's initiative, that may be the seeds of our future deliberate strategies, will come only if we create a free and open internal market. Liberty is the seed-bed of creativity.

Just as planned economies have failed disastrously everywhere they have been applied, so planned organizations will meet the same fate. And attempts to "organize" freedom, just like attempts to "organize" a free market, will meet an unsuccessful conclusion. The most that nations can do is create the playing field: the rule of law, human and civil rights, open markets, and democracy as a means to select good leaders and kick out the bad ones.

Organizations can do no more. The most we can hope to do in an organization is to create an environment in which freedom can flourish; when we do this, we know we have done the best we can to ensure future prosperity. One of John Kotter's "constants of leadership" is "the ability to create conditions that energize and inspire people to get off their fannies."

"Playing field" is not a bad metaphor for an organization. There are some agreed-upon ideas: We are playing this game and not others, we agree on the boundaries of the field, we accept some rules to make the game fair and more enjoyable (not to restrict play).

We are surely overfocused on being focused and underfocused on being playful—not silly, but play-ful. "Work tends to be a convergent activity, focusing in on the task at hand. Play is a divergent activity. It opens out and is not easy to contain."[4] We can be so serious and focused that we miss the context of the problem itself. We miss a host of possible solutions that are outside of our focus. We miss the fact that the problem is really an opportunity to explore, or that it isn't the right problem, or that it isn't a problem at all.

In addition, we miss the crucial fact that for more and more people, the lines between work and play (not office and home) are, can, and should be blurred. Surely we are an advanced enough economy and society to make work enjoyable, even playful—not as a right, but rather as an opportunity. Every job has its drudgeries, but when the job itself is drudgery—when there is no way to redeem it, improve it, make it even slightly pleasurable—the time has come to fix it, break it up, or automate it. The death of the possibility of passion in a job is the death of the imagination of the person doing it.

The Nonrational Labors of Imagination

Imagination explores, expands, and synthesizes.

Imagination conjures up ideas that could not be arrived at by reason alone. It connects concepts that reason could not connect, and may not even be able to understand. It is driven by passion to step out of the routine and mundane and operate, for at least a moment, at a higher level.

The differences between imagination and reason are shown in Table 5.1. Imagination strategizes at the deepest level when it is synthesizing widely diverse, even apparently contradictory, data. Its nonrational response is to do what only human beings can do: Create a whole new concept out of practically nothing. It forces reason out of its penchant for the linear (A to B to C) and forces a struggle with ambiguity and uncertainty. If it is not rooted in and developed by our rational faculties, imagination can become detached from reality and tend toward the irrational.

Table 5-1   The Nonrational Labors of Imagination

	The Form	The Function	Nonrational Response	Rational Response	Irrational Response
Imagination	Strategy	Synthesis	Creative	Nonlinear	Possible
Reason	Planning	Analysis	Minimal	Linear	Possible

Reason plans at the deepest level when it is analyzing, discarding the "irrelevant" (imagination's food), focusing ever more narrowly, bringing the work to "closure." Its nonrational response is usually minimal: Passion can produce a great plan, but seldom will a rational plan produce passion. The process is linear, mathematical, precise. If it is not attached to the core of who we are as human beings, it, too, can tend toward the irrational.

At our most sublime level, we are creative and imaginative beings.

Sadly, people in many organizations never have even a single sublime moment. There is no freedom, no liberty, no environment to enable people to fly.

The Death of Determinism

Determinism in all its guises is dead.

Whether it takes the form of a predetermined future state, a predictable set of future conditions, a genetically or environmentally imposed and undeniable course, or a personal spiritual conclusion that cannot be avoided or denied, determinism is a dead (and deadening) doctrine.

I have heard it said that every organization is perfectly designed to get the results it is now getting, and this is certainly true. But this doesn't mean that the organization has to be that way or stay that way. If we change the design—if we alter our decisions and actions today—we can change the results, change the future.

The future is not some fixed point that controls us and that we have to try to figure out and anticipate. The future is ours to make, ours to create, ours to change. We must get out—break out—of control and try new and strange things. We have to unleash the awesome creative power that exists only in human beings.

We won't get there based on what we know or can learn. I can know I need to lose weight, and even know how to do it, but until I am passionate about it, until I desire it and am willing to throw myself into it, I will never lose and keep off any weight. Rationality can guide and support passion, but it can't order it, predict it, or control it—not if we want to be effective and not just efficient.

Rationality means one electric utility, not five (the rationale that gave us utility monopolies), even though five competitive organizations might be more efficient and give us a better deal. Rationality means one power center in our organizations, not ten or a hundred— or as many as we have people. If we have as many passionate people as we have people, we are unstoppable and will create our own healthy future.

People today are street-smart and determined to live a meaningful life and control their own destinies. The really good ones won't abide the one central power that monitors and controls all. "For more than six hundred years, no society has had as many centers of power as the society in which we now live," says Peter Drucker.[5] Governments struggle to try to manage it all, to no avail. We will fare no better in our organizations.

Decisions made by others—investors, customers, suppliers, communities, governments—will, of course, lead to certain consequences and affect our future course. But our decisions—in response to decisions made by others, in spite of decisions made by others, outside of the decisions made by others—will lead to other consequences.

There is no destiny, except the one we make.

Passion Capital

We can measure physical capital pretty well. We can guess at our intellectual capital. But we can only imagine our passion capital. It is the most important, and the hardest to measure.

Capital is wealth. Like all wealth, passion capital—when it is properly deployed—can add value and produce more wealth.

Passion gets real, bottom-line results. When people are unleashed and given the information and resources they need, they will make the results better.

Several years ago, Hallmark Cards went through a major North American expansion program involving plants, distribution centers, offices, parking garages, and retail space. A team was formed to make it happen—on time, on budget, of high quality, as conceptualized and designed. There was no existing group capable of managing the project, so this was that rare opportunity to build a passionate team from scratch. Only people who were passionate about their work and about the program were hired.

The team threw out the rulebooks and focused instead on a clear vision and stretch goals. Projects completed in the preceding years had always been late (sometimes horribly so); this team completed every project on time and a number of them ahead of schedule. Budget overruns were the 100 percent rule before; the passionate team finished all projects under budget—sometimes by millions of dollars. The quality of prior work had been incredibly bad (the worst case being the Hyatt Regency Hotel in Kansas City, where untested suspended skywalks collapsed, killing hundreds); the new team set high standards of quality for less money—and all with an impeccable safety record.

Hallmark is a fine company, but it didn't know what to do with this team. Joyce Hall, the founder, had been a passionate man, but decades of rational planning and structuring had turned his passion into a benign, paternalistic, chain-of-command, politically oriented, play-by-the-rules company. And if this rigidification could happen in an organization that sells creativity—in greeting cards and other "social expression" products—then none of us are safe.

This was another version of the struggle at General Motors between GM proper and its fired-up Saturn subsidiary. Saturn was built on a different set of principles from the linear, logical, rational planning behemoth that General Motors has become. Saturn chose to ignite the fire and be one with its employees, whereas GM chose to quench the fire and be at war with its employees. Just as China doesn't know what to do with (or even make of) Hong Kong, so GM is uncertain and befuddled over Saturn.

Hallmark had passion capital in its new maverick team. As this book is being written, GM still has it in Saturn. And China in Hong Kong. If nurtured, or just left alone, these passionate smaller components can win in their arenas, and can bring life to the larger organizations so that they can win in their arenas.

But while passion capital will triumph externally, it can be wasted within the organization. Control is often the weapon of choice. The Hallmark team was boxed in. GM continues to rein in Saturn. And China could crush Hong Kong slowly or in the blink of an eye.

Passion capital is easier to destroy than it is to measure.

Passion Direction

Although passion can't be controlled, it can be guided and directed.

The foundational principles are agreed-upon vision and mutual trust, which we will look at in detail in Chapter 13. You will see there that we are not talking about some pie-in-the-sky, smarmy vision or a trust built on platitudes and speeches, but about down-to-earth, solid, practical principles.

We can unleash the passion, and it will still walk by our side.

Conclusion

We have to use our own passion as leaders to inflame the passions of others, not to quench their spirits. Regardless of our personalities, we have to find a way to unleash our own passions and to welcome the "leaping lightning" into our organizations.

I hate apathy and lethargy and deadness around me, and I bet you do too.

Bring on the fire.

Notes

1. For a full treatment of the devastating power of illusions in organizational life, see my book *Fatal Illusions: Shredding a Dozen Unrealities That Can Keep Your Organization From Success* (New York: AMACOM, 1997).
2. Warren Bennis and Patricia Ward Biederman, *Organizing Genius: The Secrets of Creative Collaboration* (Reading, Mass.: Addison-Wesley Publishing Company, Inc., 1997), p. 29.
3. Thomas A. Stewart, "The Man in the Gray Flannel Suit?" *Fortune*, March 16, 1998, p. 79.
4. Jerry Hirshberg, *The Creative Priority: Driving Innovative Business in the Real World* (New York: HarperBusiness, 1998), p. 116.
5. Peter F. Drucker, *Managing in a Time of Great Change* (New York: Truman Talley Books/Dutton, 1995), p. 92.

PART II

A PASSIONATE PEOPLE

Throughout history, people have, in the main, wanted to make a difference. They have wanted to be part of some overarching project or goal. They have wanted success in all areas of their lives. And they have wanted to live out in some way who they are at the core and why they believe they were put on this planet. Many have been prevented from doing so. Perhaps even more have prevented themselves.

This section looks at these key issues, which are so important to the effective use of intellectual and passion capital in a world that has moved far beyond the lower levels of Maslow's hierarchy of needs. We will see that the best leaders in the next century will use the dynamo of their people's passions to drive the engines of innovation and re-creation.

These leaders will know, as the old American proverb says, that "the road to the head lies through the heart."

6

Clues to the Presence of Passion

Emotion and passion was taboo [in the 1980s], although if you look back into history, you see that passion, vision, and mission was a good thing. We will see human emotions brought back into management.

—C.K. Prahalad, author and strategy expert

When I talked to a potential new player, I'd look him right in the eye and watch him respond to my questions. Numbers are important, but heart is as important to me. I want to know about attitude and intelligence and the ability to take it.

—Bill Parcells, professional football coach

To business that we love we rise betime,
And go to 't with delight.

—William Shakespeare, *Antony and Cleopatra*

Everyone is passionate about something, even if it's as mundane as stamp collecting or prime-time sitcoms. It's impossible to be alive and not care about *something*. The most important questions facing us as leaders are: "What is this person sitting in front of me passionate about?" and "Can this passion be directed for the good of our organization?" "Every man—even the most cynical—has one enthusiasm—he is earnest about some one thing. If there is a skeleton—there is also an idol in the cupboard!" wrote playwright John Oliver Hobbes. It's crucial that we ask these questions before hiring, promoting, or powersharing. The limitations of employees who are "dead from the neck up" are well-documented. But placing people in positions where they feel dead from the neck down, at least while they're at work, is just as unsatisfactory. (It's also crucial that we ask these questions of ourselves. Why would we want to waste our precious time doing something we don't care about?)

In order to answer these questions, we have to be able to recognize the existence of passion and discern the goals toward which it is directed. In this chapter, we'll look at some factors that make passion come to life. These include:

- willingness to confront reality
- ability to discern the truth about who we are and what we want and need
- capacity to transform information and knowledge into wisdom
- alignment between personal and organizational aspirations
- desire to make a difference
- love for labor
- indignation over conditions
- evidence of battle scars
- an amateur's orientation
- being young at heart

Each of these factors is an important clue to the presence of passion. We can't put into a person what isn't already there. We can't create passion for our organization and its values where there is no latent passion—we're just not that powerful. But we can discern a passion that is lying there, waiting to be activated, energized, directed, and fulfilled. There are important questions to be asked and answered (we discuss them in each section, and then summarize them in Table 6-1 at the end of the chapter).

Motivational programs won't generate passion. When passion replaces motivational schemes—when the fire in the belly is more important to us than the program in the manual—we will at last have arrived at an irresistible organizational life.

Willingness to Confront Reality

Many people associate passion with an unrealistic attitude: "Sure, you're all fired up right now, but you don't know the obstacles in your path. You're just not being reasonable."

There is some truth to this argument. Many people are zealous about ideas or plans that are completely unrelated to any doable reality. All utopian schemes, in which a messianic state or power is going to right all wrongs and create perfect justice, equality, and opportunity, are doomed to failure, regardless of the enthusiasm of their supporters. Since life keeps getting in the way, millions of obstacles (read: people) are slaughtered on the altar of the "vision." In Armenia, the Ukraine, the Third Reich, the Soviet Union, Cambodia under the Khmer Rouge, and the totalitarian monolith of today's (but not modern) China, commitment and enthusiasm for producing a heaven among the living have produced a living hell instead.

Businesses are not safe from this "human capacity to dismiss reality," as Jean-François Revel calls it.[1] Our tendency to do this is why Max DePree, the former president of Herman Miller, Inc., said that the first mission of a leader was to define reality. I am suggesting an even deeper, more fundamental need: The first mission of a leader is to *confront* reality.

As I have done research for my books, I have become more and more convinced that confronting reality is the starting place for success.[2] Leaders and entire organizations can and do determinedly refuse to face reality. For some, only excruciating pain (like massive market deterioration or major financial losses) will clear their focus, often when it is too late to do anything about it. Others are so resistant that they never acknowledge reality and go down with the ship.

We can refuse to acknowledge the viability of a new product (as some automakers did with minivans and sport utility vehicles). We can ignore something because we consider it a fad when it isn't a fad (as the big three U.S. automakers did with both small and imported vehicles). We can fight battles from old wars and kill ourselves in the present (as the United Auto Workers have done for decades). All of this resistance can appear quite passionate.

But here is the error: In all of these cases and more, *it isn't the passion that produces the distortion. It is the distortion, once believed and accepted as fact, that produces the negative passion.* To say it another way, it takes a substantial amount of energy to continue to believe in and act on an idea that is in direct conflict with reality. The more reality collides with our perception (and perception is *not* reality—reality is reality), the more energy it takes to keep the illusion alive. Illusions can produce an almost boundless passion—until reality finally comes flooding in and sweeps it all away.

But a passion that builds value rather than destroying it always (always) has to be based on reality. The more closely the idea, strategy, or plan is aligned with reality, the more our passion can have an impact and the more effective the implementation will be.

So dismiss the pathologically passionate. Healthy passion begins with a willingness to confront reality. It is only when people have faced reality, acknowledging both its beauty and its ugliness, that they can use it to their advantage.

How will we know that the passion we see in others and in ourselves is rooted in reality rather than in illusion? Healthy passion is usually present when people:

- Can admit that they have made a number of serious mistakes, and can articulate clearly and confidently why they are more powerful people as a result.
- Can easily and specifically describe their weaknesses, and can explain their strategy for minimizing the impact of those weaknesses.
- Can thoroughly describe and illustrate their strengths, and can explain their strategy for maximizing the impact of those strengths.
- Have a good problem-solving approach, including defining the problem, finding viable options, implementing solutions, and measuring these solutions' effectiveness.
- Can admit the specific ways in which they have contributed to their own problems and refuse to play the victim and scapegoat others or to cave in to self-contempt.
- Can explain how they have learned to feed opportunities and starve problems.
- Have a grasp of when to follow schedules and budgets and when to discard them.
- Talk freely about their openness to honest assessments.

And here's the key: When they describe these things, how do they do it? What's their pulse? Has reality beaten them? Have they been down but refused to be counted out?

Few things are more powerful in terms of developing character and passion than having had a brutal beating or two and rising above it. "Anything that does not kill me makes me stronger," said Nietzsche. What have these people made of their reality, of their experience? Has it killed them? Or has it made them stronger?

When you hear someone say, "It just wasn't fair" or "I just don't understand how they could have responded like that," and use these feelings as an excuse to deny the reality that *life is often not fair,* you're not talking to the right person. People will mistreat us, betray us, cheat us, abuse us, and all *just because we are alive.* Mistreatment comes with being human. It will stop only when we're dead—and sometimes our adversaries don't even stop then, as witness the "revisionist" biographies that desecrate a long-dead giant because (surprise) he or she had flaws.

No baloney. When you hear that in a person, you've got the first requirement for healthy passion.

Ability to Discern the Truth About Who We Are and What We Want and Need

It takes a driving passion for people to go through the incredibly difficult process of examining their lives.

Most people don't do it. "Men occasionally stumble over the truth," said Winston Churchill, "but most of them pick themselves up and hurry off as if nothing had happened." These people direct their passion at outer activities, like music and sports and movies—activities that distract rather than direct. These people get all wrapped up in the unimportant so that they never have to face the most important questions of life: Who am I? What do I need? What do I want?

Frankly, we generally do a terrible job of encouraging our children to ask these questions. We latch onto one of their passing interests or a class that they have excelled at in school, and we start pushing them to pursue it: "Maybe you ought to think of that as a career." This is the career equivalent of driving down the road with the intention of marrying the first attractive, eligible person you meet. Rational "relational tools" won't save us from a passionless marriage.

Forget all the interview questions about background, experience, etc. Forget a complex career-development questionnaire. Ask three questions and learn where someone's passions are:

"Who are you?"

"What do you need?"

"What do you want?"

"I don't know," "That's an interesting question," and "I'll have to think about it" are the wrong answers. I've heard young people—very young people—give thoughtful and thought-provoking answers to these questions. It's not a matter of age or experience. It's a matter of interest, of what a person is passionate about.

And the clue is, is this person passionate about what is going on inside himself or herself?

Capacity to Transform Information and Knowledge Into Wisdom

In our "wired" world, almost everyone picks up a lot of information, and maybe even some knowledge. The question is, is the person doing anything with it?

Wisdom is applied truth. It involves taking what we have learned and turning it into something useful and value-adding, in the fullest possible meaning of the term *value*. We'll know that we're in the presence of healthy passion when the person has learned wisdom in:

• *Self-management.* The hardest person to manage is always oneself. This is why some of the most out-of-control people are some of the biggest control freaks. We have to control something—if it's not ourselves, then it has to be someone else. Does this person know how to prioritize, how to plan, how to focus, how to let go, how to rest?

• *Relationships.* The English novelist E. M. Forster reminds us that connection is everything. How does this person connect with others? Is she capable of reaching out to others in a meaningful way? Does he know that networking doesn't mean politics and manipulation? Is she interested in serving others and meeting the needs of internal and external customers? What does he say about relationships without being prompted?

• *Persistence.* Does she know when to pursue and when to give up? Does she know when to cut her losses and when to fight for the victory that is waiting just beyond the apparent loss?

Information is plentiful, even overwhelming. Much knowledge is out there for the taking. But look for people to hire and promote who have worked to find a way to apply it in new, interesting, and meaningful ways.

Alignment Between Personal and Organizational Aspirations

Passionate people are interested in finding a "kindred-spirit" organization, not just a good job.

To put it bluntly, there is no way to get people excited about an organizational vision that they inherently don't care about. Rewording it won't help. Money won't do it. Exhortation and motivational programs won't make a difference. If they don't care about the reason your organization exists, you can forget about trying to "motivate" them later. They will never be contributors to your passionate organization.

To quote the old proverb, "You can't put in what God's left out."

This is why so much hiring and promoting is wrong-headed. We try to find "good people" (and we often don't even do a decent job of that), and then hope to get them turned on to our vision. Forget it. We need to turn our hiring and promoting practices into the painstaking process of finding the pieces that fit into our puzzle. We must do more than align people with jobs that match their own personal values and interests and abilities, although this is certainly critical. We must align them with *our* values and interests and abilities. Or rather, we must make sure that they come predisposed to align with these things.

The same is true for those with whom we choose to powershare. Alignment with who we are, where we are going, and what we want to become creates the environment in which freedom and passion can flourish and management can disappear.

A word of caution: We are *not* talking about trying to hire drones or clones. We don't want an organization populated with look-alike, think-alike, sound-alike androids. Quite the contrary: We want to build a widely diversified and widely decentralized organization populated with passionate mavericks, whose only similarity is commitment to a clearly understood and compelling vision and its supporting passions (values and interests) and core competencies (abilities).

All of this presupposes, of course, that we know what our values and interests and abilities are as an organization. Not many companies have articulated these things clearly. But once we've done that, we have to work very hard to make sure that no one walks through the door or advances through the ranks who won't fight to the death for our vision—*because it already belongs to them.*

How will we know?

There are many ways, many tools. The best tool is time. I have known dozens of leaders who have shaved time off the selection process and then spent a large multiple of the time they saved dealing with the problems—coaching, counseling, disciplining, wringing their own hands, wanting to wring the other person's neck. "A patient person is better than a warrior," says an old Hebrew proverb. The alternative is another proverb: "Marry in haste, repent at leisure."

Other tools can help. Really good testing (for values, interests, performances, etc.) can eliminate a lot of mismatches. In-depth, well-prepared interviewing by multiple people, followed by intense and passionate conversation among the interviewers, is a must. Simulations can be useful in places, as can job "shadowing" (letting someone follow a current employee for a day or more, perhaps even doing some of the work).

One tool I use for key positions is a type of 360-degree review. This is an evaluation form that the prospective employee can give to previous employers, coworkers, professors, friends, pastors, etc. It is not a performance evaluation, but rather a "who is this?" evaluation, looking at the person's values, interests, and abilities. The forms are returned directly to us by the evaluators. The prospective employee picks the evaluators, so we avoid legal hassles. It takes time. A mismatch takes more.

Another tool I use for critical positions is to have applicants or candidates for promotion write a short essay, no longer than 500 words, that tells in detail why and how their personal aspirations line up with our organization's vision, values, and core competencies, and how these would be lived out in the new job. If people don't have a rough idea of what these are when they first come in, pass—unless the first thing they do is ask about them. If they haven't or don't take the time to find out who we are, they're just looking for a job. How will we find passion there?

Five hundred words should be a piece of cake, if they really care.

Desire to Make a Difference

"How will we be different in five years if we hire, develop, or promote you?"

Listen closely to the answers to this question.

The right answers can come in many forms, but the really important ones will include how the organization's aspirations will be enhanced and achieved. Especially interesting would be answers that talk about how those aspirations might be modified or extended into new directions.

The wrong answers would be shallow ("We would be more profitable, successful, etc."), absorbed with the self ("what I would be doing is . . ."), or contrary to (not outside of) our aspirations.

We will elaborate more on this desire in Chapter 9. But we have to make sure that the raw material is there.

Love for Labor

Listen for clues in their comments about what excites them.

If it is hobbies, we don't have a connection—unless what they do in their hobby is what we need to have them do for us.

The real question is, are they excited about the stuff they are, or will be, or might someday be doing for us? This is where the real motivation is. Getting people motivated about work when they would rather be at the beach or fishing or whatever is hopeless. If they already love the work, we won't have to motivate them. All we'll have to do is make sure we don't screw up their motivation. "I never did a day's work in my life," said the inventor Thomas Edison. "It was all fun."

Walk job candidates around the office or plant. Let them spend time with people who work in other areas. See if they ask more than courteous or superficial or token questions. See if they are "hooked." Only if they love this kind of work will they be passionate in the long run.

Key questions for people:

"What turns you on about your work?"

"What excites you about our organization?"

"Why are those things exciting for you?"

"What would you like to do more of?"

"How could we work together to develop you in these areas?"

And if you're not doing what you love, for God's sake (and yours, and your organization's) get out. Even if you're sixty, even if you've done it a long time, even if you don't know where to start. As the "Chief" said to U.S. Marshall Cahill (John Wayne) about Cahill's restoring his relationship with his sons, "There ain't nothing too late, if you love it."

Indignation Over Conditions

"The problem that infuriates you the most is the problem God has assigned you to solve," says Mike Murdock.[3] Charles Dickens said that he never wrote anything unless he was angry about the subject.

Are you furious that many working people can't afford quality health care? Go into health care and attack the problem. Are you angry that minorities don't always compete on a level playing field? Attack the playing field, while you also teach the minorities to think like majorities and stop defeating themselves. Are you indignant that professional politicians seem like self-serving hacks? Run for office, join a principled campaign, write some letters. Do you hate the local schools? Find others who agree and work together to change it or start a new school. Are you sick of businesses that give lousy service? Focus on service in your own business and drive those others from the market (as Southwest Airlines and a few others have been doing for years to the major airlines, who are right now some of the worst service businesses going).

So here's the question to ask: "What makes you really mad?"

If they say, "Nothing," they're dead. Cancel the rest of the interview and call 911. The same thing goes for "I don't know" and "I'm not sure." If someone's answers are about pet peeves (people who come in late, people who don't give two weeks' notice, suppliers who change shipping dates and forget to tell us), assume that this is a petty person and move on (it's not that these issues are unimportant; they just shouldn't be given a first order of importance).

Listen instead for the voice of honorable indignation:

> "It drives me nuts when I see managers abuse people verbally and criticize them in public."

> "I hate it when people hear a new idea and either squelch it or take credit for it themselves."

> "When I hear about people downsizing without looking for

alternatives to smashing the lives of thousands of people, I want to throw up."

"I want to run from the room when I hear people start to chatter about and run down people who aren't there."

"When people are given responsibility without authority— enough rope to hang themselves—and then are blamed for failure by management, I want to kick something."

Be careful, though, if all of the person's concerns are pointed downward—complaints about workers, unions, anyone below her or him in the power structure. First, it isn't honest; this person is carefully shielding you from being insulted about your own management or organizational structure. But second, the unidirectional focus is too limited—the person's passion, over time, could be directed toward squeezing the troops.

Evidence of Battle Scars

Show me the money, nothing.

Show me the scars.

The only way to avoid serious wounds is to avoid serious battles. If we've got passion, there are times when we just have to go to war: for a new product or service, a customer who is getting slighted, a supplier who is getting stiffed, or an employee who is being treated unfairly. We may even have to fight over basic issues of integrity, honesty, and ethics.

We may win the battle, or we may lose. But either way, we'll come out of it with some wounds. When we stand up for something, a whole battalion of people may try to knock us down. The longer and harder we fight, the more and deeper the wounds.

But we're looking for scars, not open wounds. Healing and moving on are important components of a mature, passionate person. Staying wounded leads to negative passion, focused on hatred, revenge, and grudge holding.

Some questions to help identify those who have benefited from their battle scars:

- Would you tell me about your three greatest fights (from the past career for new hires and from the past year for current employees)?
- Are you glad you had the fight? Would you do it again?
- What would you do differently the next time?
- What have you learned about when, where, and how to fight?
- What were you tempted to learn that was not helpful?
- What issues or situations led you to put on your battle gear?
- What did you contribute to the problem, the wounds, or the loss?

The last question leads to one more important point: We're not talking about scars from self-inflicted wounds. We're looking for people who fight for good causes, not people who like war.

An Amateur's Orientation

Ironically, even when we are passionately committed to a cause, our passion can evaporate as we focus on it and take our expertise about it to high, even professional levels.

Passion in a field of endeavor is kept alive by looking at the field from a constantly fresh perspective. If I am an engineer, what do architects say about engineers? How about psychologists? Anthropologists? Historians? Novelists? What kind of lives have some notable engineers lived? Only by reframing my field can I keep any perspective over time.

Few things are as deadening as ponderous expertise. *"Drinking from diverse wells* has maintained [our] posture of skilled, open, and enthusiastic amateurs rather than narrow experts and tired pros," says Nissan design leader Jerry Hirshberg. "And it has led to the realization that a little bit of knowledge about a lot of subjects is a dangerously creative thing."[4] No matter how much we know, there's always much more to know, and an infinite variety of methods by which to know it.

My suggestion is that you ask: "What do you know about your field of expertise?" And listen to the *tone* of the answer. Is it all-knowing? Totally certain? Just a little too smooth?

And then come the follow-up questions: "What do you *not* know about your field of expertise? What makes you nervous? Leaves you feeling unsure?"

And then the kicker: "How would you go about expanding your grid?"

An amateur does it just for the love of it. There's no hard, cold professionalism, no arrogance (but maybe a little cockiness—"I can learn anything," or in the words of the drummer in the movie *That Thing You Do,* "I AM SPARTACUS"). What I know is fun, what I don't know is fun, the learning is fun.

I hope I never know it all.

Being Young at Heart

The late Frank Sinatra told us in song that even fairy tales would come true for us if we chose to stay young on the *inside.*

Well, maybe not fairy tales, but a damned exciting life is sure possible.

In *Organizing Genius,* Warren Bennis and Patricia Ward Biederman suggest that great teams are often made up of young people. Their thought is that as we get older, the challenges of life make us into realists who no longer can see all of the possibilities or believe we can climb all of the mountains. They're right.

And they're wrong.

They're right because life really can sap the passion right out of us. It *does* sap the life out of many of us. Nothing is more deadly than when we come to the point of saying things like "That won't work," "We'll never get that off the ground," "We've already tried that," and "We've always done it this way and it's worked." "No one is so old as he who has outlived enthusiasm," said American author and philosopher Henry David Thoreau.

This means in practice that we shouldn't overload our teams with age and experience. We should give young people who have idealism and passion (life has already sapped even a lot of young people, who are old before their time in all the wrong ways) more opportunity sooner, more chances for early leadership, more involvement in the key stuff (balanced with an appropriate apprenticeship).

But Bennis and Biederman don't go far enough. They're wrong because some people don't grow old (even though their bodies are wearing out, and they will die). The key is to avoid dying before you die. Some people have figured this out. George Burns did. Peter Drucker has given me a vision for my next forty years. (I recently got to tell him so.) We need to ask older people (anyone over twenty), "How do you intend to keep yourself young—in mind and heart, not just in body?"

Table 6-1   Clues to the Presence of Passion

Clue to Passion	Questions to Ask
Willingness to confront reality	• What serious mistakes have you made, and how are you a more powerful person because of them? • What are your weaknesses, and how do you intend to minimize their impact? • What are your strengths, and how do you intend to maximize their impact? • How do you feed opportunities and starve problems? • How do you know when to follow schedules and budgets and when to discard them? • How have you contributed to your own problems?
Ability to discern the truth about who we are and what we want and need	• Who are you? • What do you need? • What do you want?
Capacity to transform information and knowledge into wisdom	• What criteria do you use to prioritize activities? • How will you relate to internal and external customers? • How will you know when to pursue and when to let go?
Alignment between personal and organizational aspirations	• What are your personal aspirations? • How do they line up with our organization's vision?
Desire to make a difference	• How will we be different in five years if we hire, develop, or promote you?

Love for Labor	• What turns you on about your work? Why? • What excites you about our organization? Why? • What would you like to do more of? • How could we work together to develop you in these areas?
Indignation over conditions	• What makes you really mad?
Evidence of battle scars	• What have been your three greatest fights? • Are you glad you had those fights? Would you do it again? • What would you do differently the next time? • What have you learned about when, where, and how to fight? • What were you tempted to learn that wasn't helpful? • What issues or situations lead you to put on your battle gear? • What did you contribute to the problem?
An amateur's orientation	• What do you know about your field of expertise? • What do you *not* know about your field of expertise? • What makes you nervous? Leaves you feeling unsure? • How would you go about expanding your grid?
Being young at heart	• How do you intend to keep yourself young—in mind and heart, not just in body?

Sinatra goes on to tell us that this attitude will bring us a lot, even if and after we've passed the century mark. In the span of millennia, how long is a hundred and five?

We can challenge ourselves, challenge our people, to derive much from a full life, to refuse to grow old, to resist being called senior citizens or any related moniker. Let other people get old and burned out, but not us: Nothing is sadder than a burned-out old (or young) person.

And nothing is more thrilling than older people who have forgotten they are old. "You are whatever age you have decided to be," said Pablo Casals in his later years, "and I have decided to be thirty." When Teddy Roosevelt was asked why he went on a death-defying journey after leaving the U.S. presidency, his answer was stirring:

"Because it was my last chance to be a boy."

Conclusion

We've summarized the questions that can give us clues to the presence of passion. Ask them. Build them into your people process. Take some time to hear and evaluate the answers. You are trying to make a connection that is more difficult than the work of a neurosurgeon. You are attempting to connect the passions of a unique organization with the passions of a unique human being. Nothing could be more difficult.

And surely, nothing could be more rewarding.

Notes

1. Jean-Francois Revel, *Democracy Against Itself: The Future of the Democratic Impulse* (New York: The Free Press, 1992), p. 142.
2. James R. Lucas, *Fatal Illusions: Shredding a Dozen Unrealities That Can Keep Your Organization From Success* (New York: AMACOM, 1997).
3. Mike Murdock, *The Leadership Secrets of Jesus* (Tulsa, Okla.: Honor Books, 1996), p. 151.
4. Jerry Hirshberg, *The Creative Priority: Driving Innovative Business in the Real World* (New York: HarperBusiness, 1998), p. 190.

7

The Role of the Soul

Faith is the highest passion in a human being. Many in every generation may not come that far, but none comes further.

—Søren Kierkegaard, *Fear and Trembling*

What is passion? It is surely the becoming of a person. Are we not, for most of our lives, marking time? Most of our being is at rest, unlived. In passion, the body and the spirit seek expression outside of self. Passion is all that is other from self. Sex is only interesting when it releases passion. The more extreme and the more expressed that passion is, the more unbearable does life seem without it. It reminds us that if passion dies or is denied, we are partly dead and that soon, come what may, we will be wholly so.

—John Boorman, *Projections*

A man cannot make a pair of shoes rightly unless he do it in a devout manner.

—Thomas Carlyle, *Letter to Thomas Erskine*

Soul and Spirituality

The very terms make many people nervous. The soul is who we really are at our core, the part of us that gives us our identity, our character, our strength. It is what makes each one of us unique, amazing, even wondrous. Our bodies come from, replicate, and share with the gene pool of our ancestors, many long dead. But our souls stand alone.

Spirituality is a fundamental aspect of human existence and a relentless driver of decisions and actions. Unrelated to any religious persuasion, denomination, or doctrine, spirituality simply means that there is much more to people than the biological goo of which they are made. Spirituality, an undeniable component of human existence, gives life to our souls.

What Does This Stuff Mean to My Organization?

"This doesn't sound like something that belongs in a leadership book," I can hear some of you saying.

The really amazing thing is that these concepts have been infrequently addressed in the literature on leadership. How can we truly lead people if we don't know what makes them people? How can we align them with our organizational goals when we deny the most important aspects of their lives? And how can we treat them as worthy and complex individuals, rather than as employees or subordinates, when we don't take time to recognize the power within them?

And, of course, we generally don't treat them as individuals in all their glory and inscrutable complexity. So we build motivational schemes for the masses. Hiring systems. Disciplinary programs. We don't stir passion, because we don't know where it's stored.

The Reality of Spirituality

Most people are open to spirituality in some guise or form. They know that life has to be more than work and play—although these are important aspects of spirituality. They know, in the words of Helen Keller, that "life is either a daring adventure, or nothing at all." They may not think about spiritual things all of the time; they may not think about them clearly when they do think about them; they may even follow spiritual impulses that are counterproductive or self-destructive. But the drive is there. To deny it is to join those who, centuries ago, declared in the face of all evidence that the earth was a flat plate at the center of the universe.

Spiritual is defined as "Of, relating to, consisting of, or having the nature of spirit; not tangible or material. . . . Of, concerned with, or affecting the soul."[1] It comes from a Latin word meaning "breath"—it is the essence of our lives, the core that distinguishes us from the inanimate world around us and, at the level of thought and feeling, from the animate world as well.

Spiritual is "not tangible or material." We can't put our hands on it, can't define it specifically or numerically. We can't see it or measure it. If we're honest with ourselves, we have to admit that we really don't know exactly what it is or what its potential can be. There's a mystery about the whole thing.

But that doesn't mean it isn't real. There is a dimension of human life that is outside of the tangible and material. Sometimes it's bad, or even evil—witness a Pol Pot or Khomeini, driven by hidden forces that defy description. Sometimes it's sublime—witness a Mother Teresa or Max DePree, operating in a realm that we long to see often, but actually see so seldom that when we do observe people working in it, they become renowned. But despite the fact that the spiritual realm is often overlooked, it is there, and it is real. To deny the reality of spirituality and its effect on our daily lives and decisions is to foster an illusion at a numbing and perhaps fatal level.

Spirituality says, with theologian John Henry Newman, "I am a link in a chain, a bond of connection between persons. . . . I shall do good, I shall do His work . . . whatever, wherever I am. I cannot be thrown away." It says, "I count." It says more—it says that I count, what I do counts, maybe, in some undefinable way, for generations.

The Red Herring of Religion

The red herring in the area of spirituality, the great big giant distraction from a meaningful approach to the deepest and best part of who we are as humans, is often religion. Although religion can be supportive of our spirituality, it can also easily misguide or devour it.

Religion is our attempt to deal in an organized way with spirituality.

Sometimes we do it well. We come up with approaches to the spiritual realm that liberate—from self-contempt, from other-centered contempt, from self-destructiveness, from the demolition of others. These healthy religious systems deal honestly with who we are and who we aren't, what we are and what we aren't, what we are capable of and what is just beyond (or way beyond) our grasp. They contain much life-changing truth, and point our spiritual impulses in a useful and elevating direction.

But religion can take us the other way as well. Where spirituality tends to elevate, religion can too easily limit us or even drag us down. It can distract us from the truth. Under the mantle of religion, Christians have killed Moslems and Moslems have killed Christians. Jews have perished in the millions, in the name of religion and because of their religion. Protestant Christians have killed Catholic Christians, and watched their own slaughtered in return. Few forces in life can wreak as much destruction as "religion" that is absent spirituality.

Religion itself isn't the problem. It's the wrong *application* of religion, the codifying and labeling and restricting and judging and condemning. It's the arrogance that claims to possess all of the answers while others have none. It's law without grace, rules without reason, temper without tempering, fervor without passion. An old German proverb says, "Marriage is heaven and hell." The same could be said of much religion.

But the charge to us as leaders is not to throw out the good with the bad, the mystery with the confusion. The truth is there and can, in fact must, be found. The spiritual impulse is there and must be recognized and dealt with. We can't afford to let the innumerable errors of countless religious systems drown out the need to tap into this ocean of passion.

My experience tells me that most people are open to spirituality but that many are closed to, bored with, or fanatical about religion. We leaders can—with great care, to be sure—appeal to their spiritual core while avoiding the red herring of religion.

Tapping Into the Spiritual Core

There is a drive today, in people of various ages, cultures, and professions to find the meaning of life, to have relationships based on something unchangeable, and to struggle to do the right thing. Organizations that help people do these things—or, as a minimum, don't place obstacles in the way—will be the ones that will attract and retain the best and brightest and most enthusiastic in the twenty-first century.

In order to tap into spirituality while avoiding the red herring of religion, we need to take the following steps.

• *We must recognize that people have spiritual values that drive their behaviors.* We may not understand these values, and we certainly may disagree with them. We accept that someone may not even know clearly what these values are or how to articulate them. But we know the values are there, and we know that they have effects, and we take them into account. We devise ways to discern these values and build them into our planning.

Someone, for example, may believe in the immense value of community. She may want to move our organization beyond simply communicating with the local communities through our public relations and lobbying departments to an organic connection with these communities at many levels. And, recognizing that surroundings do matter, she might want our internal environment to resemble a vibrant small town more than a sterile hospital ward. We should listen when she talks about community, not just to let her know that she is being heard and respected, although that is good, but because we know that she is bringing something very valuable to the table. If we let people's positive spiritual values in, they will permeate our organization and, in some wonderful transfer, become our values, too.

• *We must make it a priority to never, ever, ask people to make decisions or take actions that conflict with their most cherished values.* That is the death of respect for our organization, and the death of passion for the individual. We cannot be passionate about an organization or mission that denies the value of what we treasure and pushes us to do what we loathe on the inside.

On several occasions, I have seen supervisors told to terminate someone for personal or political reasons with which the supervisor did not agree. The death of the passion in that supervisor is much costlier than the salary of the person who was terminated. The supervisor was forced to either fight the order or lose self-respect. Leaders need to give their people choices, but not this kind.

• *We need to pay attention both to what people think (the rational reaction) and to what they feel (the emotional/spiritual reaction).* All too often, we try to "sell" our people on a new program or idea. We lay it all out, point by point, and believe that we've addressed the whole person when we've really only addressed a fraction—probably, in many cases, the least important fraction. The feelings—the visceral, emotional, spiritual reactions to the program or idea—may not even be clear, though the reaction itself is strong. It may take weeks or months before the full spiritual reaction is clear.

Whenever I introduce a new idea, program, or initiative, I allow people to "sound off" then and there. But I always try to revisit the issue, perhaps several times, partly to get more ideas but mostly to give the feelings and passions an outlet. We can easily be deceived into thinking we have buy-in because people say, "I agree," and, "I can see the logic of what you're saying." They can give us all sorts of analytical and rational responses without ever even hinting at the volcanic reaction going on inside.

- *We ask ourselves the hard-to-answer question, "How can we connect their values to ours?"* How can we turn a desire to serve others into better customer service? How do we turn a desire to right wrongs into better handling of customer complaints? How do we transform a desire to build relationships into a demolition of departmental and personal barriers? Once we understand the values, some time and care and attention are all that are needed to creatively incorporate those values into our organization's soul.

- *We can make passion a major factor in our decisions.* At the level of individual decision making, we are never on a higher plane than when we are driven by and follow our passions. "Several years ago, I discovered the key ingredient in any decision-making process: passion," says Disney Channel president Anne Sweeney. "If you let passion inform your decisions, you'll make good ones."[2] This is so because passion is spiritual; it is *who we are,* while reason tells us what we *ought* to be.

The same is true for organizational decision making. There are key questions: Which direction stirs the most passion? Why shouldn't we go there? If this other plan is so great, where is the passion? What will keep it going when it encounters the inevitable obstacles, if nobody cares? Few organizations make passion the key ingredient in the decision-making process. We can take the lead in this cutting-edge approach.

- *We can give people a direct outlet for their spiritual impulse.* We can provide a forum within the organization in which they spend so much of their lives where those who are dealing with catastrophic illness or other bigger-than-me problems can find some help. The help doesn't have to be financial. When we're in trouble, just knowing that people genuinely notice and care and will continue to do so makes mere money fade into the background.

The point is not to do these things in lieu of church or temple or personal spiritual development, but rather in addition to them. Why should this important dimension of our personhood be excluded from our careers and our organizations? In a sense, all of life is spiritual, and at the end the spiritual is the only thing that really counts.

Things to Avoid

Some things should be avoided when dealing with the spiritual impulse. Even if we don't take the actions listed in the preceding section, we must at a minimum avoid offending people in the following ways.

Religious Jargon

When organizational leaders talk about being "born again," they may have the best of intentions and even an excellent point. Many organizations do indeed need to be "born again," probably every decade or two (or more frequently). The problem is that the phrase means too much to some of the hearers and too little to the others. Some will mistake organizational regeneration for a spiritual crusade, and cause it to founder by making it something that it cannot be. Others will resent the cheap use of words that are very meaningful to them personally, bringing the sublime to bear on the mundane. Some will even perceive the phrase to be hypocritical or manipulative. We need to talk about the principles, but to avoid words that already carry other—and perhaps religious—overtones (for example, "our ten commandments," "singing from the same hymn book," or "it will be a real revival meeting").

One manager I knew (and he was a manager with not a shred of leadership about him) had a penchant for talking and writing about love. He had picked up the idea of "loving your fellow man" in church and absorbed it into his management arsenal. What he meant was, "Loving me means doing exactly what I say." People resented—and laughed behind his back at—his use of words that he didn't mean.

The Bully Pulpit

We need to make sure that neither we nor any of our leaders use the organization as a forum for our personal religious doctrines, beliefs, or practices, *as far as others around them are concerned.* It is very difficult to believe deeply in something and not want everyone around us to believe in it as well. But the essence of good organizational practice—as well as a key principle of religious freedom—is that no one uses his or her position or power to make others fall in line on such matters. Meditation can be terrific as a personal practice, but it can be terrible in its organizational life form.

Interference

We have to ensure that our expectations are not so all-consuming that people have no time left to pursue and fulfill their spiritual impulse. We can learn the rhythm of their lives, their church or temple meeting times and responsibilities, and do all we can not to interfere. We should make this effort, not because it will keep us out of legal trouble about discrimination, but because it is brilliant.

Critique

Finally, we should be extremely careful not to say things related to spirituality that will unnecessarily offend people. We've already talked about using religious jargon, but more general critiques of religion can also be offensive. Because the spiritual impulse is so very central, it is also very sensitive.

I once sat in on a discussion of how to avoid trying to keep a product alive against all marketplace reality. One person, attempting to draw a parallel, said, "Yes, we don't want to be like those religious nuts in Waco." A couple of people in the room were offended—*not* because they were anything like the people in Waco, but because they considered themselves to be religious and thought that this important component of their lives was somehow being dismissed or ridiculed. It wasn't a suable offense, but that doesn't mean it wasn't an offense.

The first rule of medicine is, "Do no harm." Regardless of our view of spirituality, we should do our people no harm.

Spiritual Intelligence

Spiritual intelligence, involving the best of what is in our personal and organizational souls, is, for the most part, an underutilized component of success and driver of change.

Danah Zohar reminds us that "all fundamental transformation is ultimately *spiritual* transformation, spiritual in the very broadest sense as issuing from the level of reflection, meaning, and value. This is true for individuals and for companies. It is crucially true that creative thinking emerges from this spiritual level."[3] We are drawing on this level when we are changing or creating, regardless of our awareness of that reality. Zohar goes on to say that "the spiritual level is the company's basic vision [which is] its overall—and often *unconscious*—sense of identity, its aspirations, its sense of itself in the wider world, its deeper, motivating core values and long-term strategies."[4]

What is this "level of reflection, meaning, and value"? What does spiritual intelligence mean in practice?

- *Reflection.* Most organizations do some form of strategic planning, but few engage in strategic *visioning* and strategic *thinking*. Once a year isn't enough. We have to reevaluate who we are and what we want to become on a continuous basis. Bad organizational decisions are usually the result of a long chain of decisions made without the benefit of reflection. The unexamined *organizational* life is also not worth living. It's not "ready-aim-fire" or "ready-fire-aim" but asking whether we are shooting in the right direction or at the right target— or whether we should be shooting at all.

- *Meaning.* Why are we really in business? To make money? It is true that making profits is to a business what breathing is to a person, but no person lives to breathe. We breathe to live, not the other way around. Profits are necessary, but they most assuredly are not sufficient to drive and motivate fundamentally spiritual beings. Some people are motivated primarily by money. I try, if at all possible, to avoid them. Few are as subtly sick as those who live for and love money.

- *Value.* We come from a vast array of religious backgrounds and persuasions. Can we possibly find some common values? Can we draw these values out from the best that is within us, rather than imposing them from above? Can we agree on the behaviors that illustrate these values in action? Finally, are we willing to put the mechanisms in place to ensure that everyone in the organization lives by these values? If not, we deny the spiritual base of our future.

We can find ways to enhance this spiritual side of our organization. We can "promote a model for business that allows people, in their daily work, to remain true to their deepest beliefs. Adopting such a model . . . will soon become the only way for companies to make a profit, because it will soon become the only way for companies to stay creative. . . . People need to believe in what they do for a living before they can tap their deepest creative potential."[5] It isn't possible to have transformational creativity without having the whole-being expression that produces it.

Organizations fail at this point more than almost anyplace else. In a recent survey, while 32 percent of respondents said that work had improved their spiritual lives, 25 percent said it had worsened it, and 36 percent said that work had had no effect one way or the other. This means that organizations are missing this crucial area with over three-fifths of employees.[6]

Conclusion

The spiritual intelligence of our organizations is nothing magical or really even very mystical. It is the sum of the spiritual intelligence of the people who make up the organization. Organizations that deny the spiritual impulse, that take no steps to utilize and enhance it, that in fact take steps to obstruct and destroy it, are, at best, spiritually dense. At worst, they are spiritually villainous. Little creativity or long-term value can come from such poor material.

People who have denied their own spiritual impulse are doomed to superficiality. The same is true of organizations. Spirituality is not everything, but neither is it nothing.

We can dare to be different.

We can dare to be spiritual.

Notes

1. *The American Heritage Dictionary of the English Language, Third Edition* (Boston: Houghton Mifflin, 1996)
2. As quoted in *Fast Company*, June-July 1998, p. 88.
3. Danah Zohar, *Rewiring the Corporate Brain* (New York: Berrett-Koehler Publishers, 1997), pp. 18–19.
4. Zohar, pp. 18–19.
5. David Dorsey, "The New Spirit of Work," *Fast Company*, August 1998, p. 128.
6. Jeffrey L. Seglin, "Americans at Work," *Inc.*, June 1998 , p. 94.

8

Commitment to a Greater Goal

The longing for transcendence [is] the desire to be part of something out of the ordinary that is good. Transcendence is what we experience in a small but powerful way when our city's football team wins the big game against tremendous odds. The deepest part of our heart longs to be bound together in some heroic purpose with others of like mind and spirit.

—Brent Curtis, author and speaker, in *Mars Hill Review*

It is remarkable that there is little or nothing to be remembered written on the subject of getting a living; how to make getting a living not merely honest and honorable, but altogether inviting and glorious; for if *getting* a living is not so, then living is not.

—Henry David Thoreau, *Life Without Principle*

A business that makes nothing but money is a poor kind of business.

—Henry Ford, founder, Ford Motors, Inc.

Should we align people's passions with our goals, or our goals with people's passions?

Yes.

We need to market our goals to our people. We need to sell them on our goals and why they are important. We need to make a pitch that will stir them to join us. We can't assume that they're going to come along for the ride. Even more important, we can't assume that their alignment isn't critical. It is critical, and it isn't a "gimme." We've got to work hard to get our people to believe in what we are doing and where we are going.

But aligning their passions with our goals isn't enough—not nearly enough. When we are asking people to work ridiculous hours on a major project, to sacrifice time with their families and other aspects of their private lives, to spend their very selves on what we need, we've got to offer something stirring in return. Money won't do it, benefits won't do it, incentives won't do it. Over the long run, even recognition won't do it.

There has to be something intrinsically valuable about the direction we are taking. When people can't sleep and start adding up ("five years at sixty hours a week—my God, I've spent fifteen thousand of my waking hours on that effort"), they have to believe—to really *believe*—that the effort was worth that piece of their lives that can never be reclaimed. We have to be humble enough, and realistic enough, and smart enough, to align our goals with their passion, if we want them to stay passionate and we want them to stay.

Internal Marketing

Internal marketing is critical.

We have to take the time to ensure that people's passions are aligned with our goals. The primary place where this occurs is in the process of matching—matching applicants with jobs, candidates with promotions, people with assignments to projects and teams.

Internal marketing won't bail out a bad match. When people are fundamentally misaligned—when their values do not match ours, their interests do not match the required work, their personal goals do not match what we are trying to accomplish—no sales pitch will get them to buy.

But even if the fundamental alignment is in place and fundamental misalignments have been corrected, we still have some work to do.

Many organizations do a less than excellent job of marketing themselves. Often, the place where marketing is most needed is *within* the organization, yet little or no marketing is done there.

At the most, we have a "communications" person or department, and maybe we put out a newsletter. But this is far from marketing. Our external customers won't get it if we don't tell them about how wonderful and useful our products or services are. How can we expect our internal customers to get it if we don't treat them as well as we treat our external customers?

For a goal to be meaningful to them, we've got to tell them what's in it for them. Doing so involves several steps:

• We have to make sure that there really is something in our goals for them. An organizational vision that reads, "Our vision is to provide a superior rate of return to our shareholders" is necessary but not sufficient. We have to provide good returns, no question. It's basic to our existence as an organization. But that won't be enough to stir the blood of our employees.

• We have to state our goals in elevating, ennobling terms that avoid sounding hokey or syrupy. This is much harder to do than it is to say. Flowery words won't wash. But these statements have to make our people *feel* something positive if they're going to get them on our side.

• We have to do some test marketing. We have to try to state our goals in terms that people can get excited about, and then we have to see if anyone actually does get excited about them. If we get yawns, we need to change the medium so that they can get the message.

• We have to find out somehow (perhaps through surveys or focus groups) how much passion our employees feel for our goals. If people aren't responding, it may be that we just haven't spent enough time or creativity in selling them. Or it may mean that our goals stink and need to be changed.

• We have to structure our marketing to reach the broadest possible audience. We must recognize that goals that meet only shareholders' needs are insufficient. Even those that include more stakeholders—customers, vendors, partners—may be inadequate. What about the nondirect stakeholders? What about our communities, which suffer when any part of their economic life declines? What about our noncustomers, all of those people who aren't buying from us today but might tomorrow? How do our goals include them? What about future generations, who can't speak for themselves and can be represented today only by our voice? Without a broad-based understanding throughout our organization of whom and what we are really serving, we will be limited and perhaps destroyed by our narrowness of vision.

• We have to understand the difference between loyalty and commitment. Organizations have expended far too much energy trying to figure out a way to kindle or rekindle the magic potion of "loyalty." Too often, what passes for loyalty from employees has been laziness or inertia rather than real commitment. The organization, on the other hand, has too often defined loyalty as "don't rock the boat" and "sacrifice your family." We can stir commitment, but we should give up the push for loyalty.[1]

• Leaders have to embody this marketing program. The best advertisement for our goals is us living them out passionately in front of our people. If we're really committed to and fired up about the goals, they won't miss it.

We shouldn't underestimate the power of an ongoing internal marketing program. Many fire-breathing, goal-oriented organizations were, in an earlier life form, flat and dull and going nowhere. Now, providing the very same products or services, they seem unstoppable. What was the difference? We can still remember powerful advertising slogans years or decades later. Why can't we have the same effect when the product is our future?

It is important—critical, absolutely necessary—that we spend real time and resources to stir the passions of our people for our vital goals. Otherwise, all we get out of them is what we can get by beating or bribing.

Pretty primitive organizational tools.

Internal Alignment

For several years, management literature has discussed the motivational nature of BHAGs (Big Hairy Audacious Goals).[2] But these goals can't be presented in a vacuum, which is what will exist inside of our people if we haven't connected these goals to their passions. Relatively few corporate goals are both widely shared and inspiring.

There are some ways in which our goals can be aligned with our people's personal ambitions to produce a higher level of true passion.

• *Rethink our current goals with some incisive questions.* Could an entry-level person make sense of this goal? Can people on the front line connect this goal to the related decisions that they have to make every day? Would the average person working here come in sick to help us meet this goal?

• *Evaluate all new goals with these questions in mind.* Make sure they will "play in Peoria" (our plants and offices) before we try to pull them off in "New York" (our management committee or board of directors). If they won't stir passion, why in the world would we want to make them part of our portfolio?

• *Let our people help us set our goals.* Sure, they don't know as much as we do, they don't have access to all of the information, they have their axes to grind, they may not be as committed as we are. We need to involve them anyway. Because without them, our plans are toast. No matter how lofty the goals we as leaders have, it is truly amazing how little power we have to carry them out.

• *Regularly have our people evaluate and rate our goals on a "passion scale."* Vince Lombardi once said, "Those who have invested the most will be the last to surrender." Nobody invests in things they don't believe in. Jettison the good ideas that nobody cares about. Sell them to someone whose people can get excited about them.

A Case Study in Alignment

I recently had the privilege of working with a *Fortune* 1000 company that was trying to pull off alignment at the deepest possible level. Potlatch Corporation, a century-old forest and paper products company, sought to align its twenty-first century goals at the core: the organizational vision.

I told Potlatch we weren't interested if the company was just going to do "the vision thing," a quick initiative designed to get some high-sounding plaques on the walls. The company heartily agreed, and told me that the desire was to have *everyone* involved from the start in the process of setting a vision, identifying core values and related behaviors, and putting structures and mechanisms in place to ensure that it all came passionately to life.

From the beginning, this was a bottom-up effort. A team of twenty-five people was chosen (by individual plants and offices rather than by top management) to represent the company's 7,000 employees. The team included various levels of front-line and middle management, and both union and nonunion hourly workers. This team was authorized by the management committee to determine and write the organization's vision statement, without interference by the committee.

The Vision Team, which we advised and guided, did an extensive survey of all employees to determine what the core values of the company were and ought to become. It then drafted a vision statement based on this survey. This vision statement addressed the core values that were identified and the problems that were most frequently mentioned. The draft vision statement was submitted to all employees for evaluation and comment, and was then revised. Team members made presentations to groups of managers, groups of employees, and even to the management committee and the board of directors. Guests at team meetings included the CEO, members of the management committee, an officer from the international union, and people from various functions (such as training).

To ensure that the vision was effectively implemented, the Vision Team prepared a guidance book that included an extensive description of behaviors that illustrated what the vision, including all the core values, would look like in practice. The team also prepared recommendations on communication of the vision, learning and development related to the vision, and means of sustaining the vision over time. These included recommendations on structures (new and revised) and on mechanisms (systems, policies, procedures, practices) that would ensure that the vision became real on the floor, to every employee. Vision steering teams were established at each site to drive the process and handle the inevitable issues and problems.

To support its recommendations, the team benchmarked numerous organizations to determine best and cutting-edge practices. The team itself did the benchmarking and related trips; we merely provided suggestions and direction.

The result? A comprehensive vision statement, covering the purpose of the organization and all critical core values, prepared and implemented by the employees themselves with support from the management committee. Employees believe in it, not because we had to work to get their buy-in, but because *it already belonged to them.* With a top-down approach, organizational leadership needs to sell the vision and eject those who don't buy. With a bottom-up process, the vision is already theirs, so the need to "sell" and "eject" is greatly reduced.

The Vision Team's motto, which was coined in answer to people's complaints about the organization, was, "We *are* Potlatch." The problems, and thus the solutions, were no longer "out there." The process came to feel like a heroic effort rather than a change initiative. I watched this team of people from different eras and worlds coalesce and come to feel closely connected as they hammered out agreements and directions. There was a like*heartedness* that kept it all together even when like*mindedness* was hard to come by. I watched as bogus barriers (between management and labor, company and union, union and nonunion) lessened in sharpness and intensity.

The team became a prototype of what could happen throughout the organization. The opening sentence of the vision statement was "Potlatch People Make It Better," and this became a watchword for the team. What do we do with this situation? We make it better.

I have never been part of, or seen, anything quite like it. As of this writing, there is still much to be done on implementation, but the alignment is there at a very basic level.

Elements of a Heroic Effort

Many different things have to fall in place before people can feel passionately committed to a greater goal. Some of these are:

- *People have to feel that the goal matters.* There has to be an awareness that the results of our efforts will have a significant impact. Will life be better if we do this well?
- *There has to be true ownership.* The mission can't be partly ours and partly someone else's. Everything else aside, is this ours to win or lose?
- *People have to believe that the goal could not be achieved without them.* Their labors, their sacrifices, their united effort is needed. Ultimately, heroic efforts are about responsibility, accountability, and duty. What will happen if we fail?
- *There has to be a sense of urgency.* Something important has to rest on the timing of the outcome. The clock is about to run out. Our competitors are about to go to market with a similar product. Do we have what it takes to win?
- *People have to understand that "great goal" doesn't automatically translate to "bigger goal."* Stretch goals are not necessarily numerical goals. Will this effort change things, even if we can't quantify it now or later?

When we as leaders create such an environment, we have set the stage for the most dramatic alignment possible.

External Alignment

There is still more that we can do.

As we have just seen, we can align the passions of our people with our goals (if our goals are worthy), and we can align our goals with their passions (if their passions are worthy). But we can also align our internal goals and passions with external goals about which our people can be passionate.

Many people for years have been taking one of two opposing positions:

"We're in business to meet our goals and make a profit."

"We should be concerned about being socially responsible."

Today, only extremists would hold just one of these positions. Most people would agree that we have to do both. Without profits, it's hard to have a positive social impact, and without social responsibility, profits are going to get harder and harder to come by. But the reality is that we can try to tie the two together as intricately as possible.

We can tie our organizational goals to greater, broader-based external goals. We can make the achievement of our goals lead directly and *automatically* to achieving other, external goals.

In other words, it is not either "just make money" or "be socially responsible," but rather "if we make money, here are the socially responsible things we can do."

"If we make $x, we will donate $y to the community hospital."

"If this department hits this production target, $z will be given to this agreed-upon worthy cause."

"Of every increase in revenue or profit, 10 percent will be plowed back into the local community/schools."

"For every hour of overtime this group works, it will be permitted to donate x minutes of paid time to help the disabled."

The most effective approach would be to let individuals, teams, departments, plants, etc., designate where the money or time goes from a range of options.

There are those who will claim that this is not the business of the organization, that this is "soft."

But what is the business of the organization? Is it to make money, or to make value? Value is the more expansive view, the more humanly beneficial view, and in the long run probably even the most profitable view. What reasonable person wouldn't want to work for— no, *commit to*—an organization where his or her passions are accounted for in the organization's internal and external goals?

This isn't soft—it's hard, it's solid, because it brings greater:

- Self-respect
- Internal respect for the organization
- External respect for the organization

Just as soft skills—communication, interpersonal relations, conflict resolution, goal setting—are really hard skills (because they are harder to master and have greater impact), so the soft skill of aligning people's passions with internal and external goals is really a very hard skill indeed. And just as the hard skills—technical training, mastery of details—are really soft skills (because they are easier to master and more easily become obsolete), so the hard skills of making money and practicing public relations are really very soft skills indeed.

Profit is not just what's left over after subtracting costs from revenues. Profit is benefit. And if it is true that we reap what we sow, the wider the sweep of our benefit to people, the greater the harvest of all sorts of profits.

Conclusion

Aligning our goals with the passions of our people is, ultimately, not just the right thing or just the smart thing.

It's the right thing because it is the smart thing, and it's the smart thing because it is the right thing.

Notes

1. For a more complete look at this topic, see my book *Balance of Power* (New York: AMACOM, 1998), especially pages 26–27 and 127.

2. See the book *Built to Last: Successful Habits of Visionary Companies* by James C. Collins and Jerry I. Porras (New York: HarperBusiness, 1994).
3. "Compassionate capitalism," in Charles Handy's phrase. We should appreciate the free market, but only one that cares about people. I don't hire those who don't.

9

The Need to Make a Difference

My sword I give to him that shall succeed me in my pilgrimage, and my courage and skill to him that can get it.

—John Bunyan, *The Pilgrim's Progress*

To contemplate the possibility that one's name and work might be remembered after one's death is uplifting. It is a way of transcending the distractions of the present and focusing on what might be important for the future . . . the possibility of creating something of lasting value can be ennobling for both the creator and the public for which it is created. And there is no reason to believe that this sense of nobility is incompatible with a responsible business outlook.

—David Finn, "The Price of Ignoring Posterity"

For what, indeed, is there in all this so slender and brief span of life, [that] may move us to such great labors, [but] that the memory of our name be not lost with life, but extended to all posterity.

—Cicero, Roman philosopher and writer

Most people want to make a difference, to leave behind some kind of legacy. The worst thought is that we were there, and it just didn't matter. We left no impression. The machine plowed ahead, taking no notice of our work. No one was changed, no one's lot was improved, what we really cared about was never heard.

There are, to be sure, some truly rotten people who deserve to be discounted and disremembered. The only difference and happiness they bring is the one sarcastically referred to by Cervantes in *Don Quixote*: "There is a strange charm in the thoughts of a good legacy, or the hopes of an estate, which wondrously removes or at least alleviates the sorrow that men would otherwise feel for the death of friends."

For the rest of us, though, we hope for much more than this. When asked what was the single most important thing that contributed to Southwest Airlines' being named by *Fortune* as the number one "Best Company to Work For," Vice President of People Libby Sartain said, "People choose to work as individuals and feel they can make a difference."[1] Not pay, not benefits, not working conditions, but one of the grandest of human drivers set them apart.

This chapter explores the need that most people feel to have their lives and time count, and how organizations can capitalize on that need.

The Need to Leave a Legacy

There is something inside of us as humans that wants to be remembered.

We know that we won't always be here—in the organization in the short run and on the planet in the long run. Faced with the crumbling and dusty ruins of once-mighty civilizations, we will probably even admit that our memory will surely fade—probably sooner rather than later. But no matter. We want to be remembered, at least by those who knew us, by our family and friends, by our own generation, by at least our own descendants, and—if we work at it and are fortunate—by many people yet unborn, in civilizations we cannot even imagine.

We don't think about this need often, perhaps. But the thought keeps coming. As we get older, it almost certainly will come more frequently and with greater force. The possibility of being forgotten becomes a great, unbearable weight. To be erased from human memory—at least its conscious memory—is like receiving a punishment, a banishment, for a crime we never committed. Being remembered is different from immortality, but it seems more tangible and at least hints at immortality. We want to leave a mark.

There are two perspectives from which we can view this idea of legacy. One is the legacy that we can leave to our organization as one of its leaders. The other is the opportunity to leave a legacy that our organization can provide to all who are willing to passionately commit to it.

The Seven Steps of a Decent Organizational Legacy

There are certainly many ways in which we could look at this crucial but too often ignored (at least in business circles) subject of legacy. We often hear that businesspeople aren't concerned about the long term; they're supposedly focused on achieving results in the very short term. This may be true for many, but not for leaders with passion and intelligence and foresight and wisdom and compassion.

There are at least seven steps we can take as leaders to leave a mark, an excellent organizational legacy.

Visualize the Impact

We can determine that in every major decision-making process, we will spend some time asking ourselves about the decision's impact in ten or twenty-five or fifty years on stakeholders who may not yet even be born. Simply asking the questions can lead to different decisions.

If, for example, we are making an acquisition, we can ask:

- What kinds of subtle or organized culture changes will this lead to?
- How will this limit our future? What restrictions will this place on our flexibility?
- What sorts of people will this require us to hire? What will they do to our culture? Are we willing to accept those changes?
- What are the likeliest reasons for our CEO in twenty years to curse us for this decision? What makes us think this acquisition will still be around?
- Will the people leading this organization in fifteen years be able to feel passion for this? Since those people may be working here right now, should we ask them?
- How can we extend the impact of their fresh perspective beyond the initial "honeymoon" phase?

It isn't that hard to visualize and get some good answers. The hard part is making the decision to ask the questions.

Expand the List of Advisors

We can bring in influences other than the "normal" mainstream advisors upon whom we as organizational leaders usually call.

- We can ask historians to give us perspective and to outline similarities to what people have done before.
- We can ask sociologists and anthropologists to present the possible unanticipated consequences of new human resource programs on the daily life of the organization.
- We can ask doctors and psychologists to advise us on the proper level of stress in the organization (too much and we disintegrate, too little and we evaporate) and what we can do to find and approximate the healthy balance.
- We can ask a writer to put together our organizational "story," complete with villains and heroes, failures and achievements, and most of all honesty and inspiration. We can then evaluate whether we like the story or want to change it.

The point is to make the impact of the decision better and greater by making those involved in it more numerous and broad-based. Bigger legacies require more and bigger participants. We just need to make sure they are passionate.

Allocate Enough Resources

We can allocate enough resources to assure that the decision will be fully and thoroughly implemented. Most leaders fall down on this point. We feel that we have won when we have made the decision, rather than when the decision has taken root and grown inside of the organization.

It can take three to six months or more for a new direction to begin to imbed itself into our organizational life. It can be years before it becomes normal—"the way we do things around here." Deciding to move in a new direction doesn't make it happen. Believing in it, supporting it, and passionately pushing it are crucial to transform it from fad into "fabric".

All important decisions about which we are passionate need to be supported by systematic follow-up. "Systematic" means that we do it at preselected intervals, and that we do it for a considerable period of time. We have to go long if we're going to go deep.

Nurture the Ideas

We can understand that nothing of value is grown in a quarter or a year. To make a dent, we're going to have to commit to an idea for a significant amount of time so that we can nurture and develop it. This doesn't necessarily mean that we as individuals commit to the same organization for all of that time—although it may. It may mean that we stay in the same industry or remain committed to the same technology, or topic, or issue.

As an organization, it means that we give ideas time to develop—a concept well known in the early days of television, for example, but applied hardly at all in our day of quick cancellations. In this sense, our wired, quick-data world can work to our disadvantage, as we have so much urgent information telling us to change course or drop a plan that resistance can appear illogical, unseasonable, even foolish. This is the counterpoint to the truth that we live in a fast-paced world where change and instantaneous decision-making are the norm.

To make a difference, we have to learn to differentiate between the 90 percent of the time that we need to move fast and the 10 percent where moving slowly is crucial and speed kills. The mantra today is "speed." But just as the society's future is dictated more by the deep, almost invisible, extended trends than by today's headlines, so our future may be formed more by the 10 percent we nurture and defend from speed than by the 90 percent where speed is king.

Staying power, the ability to win over the long haul, to still be fighting when others have moved on—this is the stuff of legacy. Only passion can provide the energy to make it so.

Select Believers

We have to surround ourselves with a lot of people who believe in two things: our idea and us. We have to have a good number of people who are committed—who believe in what we are doing and want to be a part of it. And we have to have a few people who are loyal—who are personally devoted to us, believe in and appreciate our abilities and potential, want all of our dreams and plans to come true, and are willing to spend themselves to make it happen. We should plan and work to get commitment from everyone around us—at a minimum, from those in key positions. We should live and hope to earn the loyalty of a few, who may have the drive to make our legacy reality even if we are unable to finish the job.

Position Properly

We have to position ourselves properly to leave a legacy. Location isn't everything, but it is very important if we want to make a difference. We may have great dreams and goals, but the organization we are in may not be big enough, may have the wrong (and unchangeable) culture, may be in the wrong geographical area or industry, or simply may not be able to surround our dream. Ernie Banks was one of the greatest baseball players who ever lived, but he spent his entire career playing for a team that never won a championship, never was even very good. His legacy is very limited, at least outside of Chicago. He wasn't able to position himself because he played in the days before free agency, when a player could move only if his team decided to trade him. But employees today are all free agents who can choose where they want to work.

This raises a critical point: Are we working where we and our ideas are celebrated, or are we merely tolerated? When we are passionate about a direction that the people around us are passionately against, a healthy battle might improve the whole organization. But at some point, as the battles turn into a Thirty Years' War, our ideas and directions and lives will drain away. There are seldom any heroes in this kind of war, and often few survivors. We don't need to volunteer for insignificance.

A great person with a great idea still needs a great place to try it out. It may not be easy to find the right culture, where individual and organizational passions match. There are factors (such as the economy, available jobs, and family considerations) that can add to the challenge. But the alternative is really ugly, because it means that our impact will be very small, if not zero.

A very bad ROI, indeed.

Prepare for Opportunity

In every life there will be opportunities for greatness. Most people, however, are not prepared to take advantage of these windows of opportunity. We usually cannot manufacture the opportunities; we have to content ourselves with the knowledge that they will come. But we can prepare ourselves to be ready when the opportunity comes, to have the skills and supporting structure to take full advantage of it. We can bide our time, be ready for our time, be alert to when our time comes. As professional golfing great Gary Player said, "The harder you work, the luckier you get." The old saying goes that luck is what happens when preparation meets opportunity.

I have spent over twenty-five years immersed in the business world, reading, making notes, preparing, so that I could write on the foundations of organizational success: the need to stop illuding and confront reality, the need to powershare and develop leaders at every level, and the need to make passion a higher priority than reason. Though I am not sure what I may write next, I am absolutely certain that I will stay immersed and continue reading, making notes, and preparing. All of us as leaders can keep working on our "book"—the formation of our personal leadership story and the power it can have to affect others for good.

If we take these seven steps, we can add another dimension to our leadership and give ourselves at least a shot at a legacy. We will probably, over time, also improve our short- and mid-term results, as our decisions take on a deeper and more enduring quality.

Legacy for All by Organizational Design

We can also take some steps to build legacy into the very design of our organizations. Doing so will give everyone who cares the opportunity to leave at least a small but passionate bequest to those who come after.

Capitalize on Inner Needs

We can capitalize on people's inner need to make a difference. This doesn't have to be expensive. A trophy room could be set up chronologically (awards and recognition on a year-by-year basis) or by topic (process improvement, customer service, cost minimization). It is important that these awards be displayed well, that the effect is not "cheesy," that the room has a sense of endurance. Preferably we can set it up in a location that doesn't change, at least not very often.

Schools and hospitals and charitable organizations have often done a good job with this approach with their members and donors. The various sports spend a lot of money on their Halls of Fame—and no matter how enjoyable those sports might be, they are probably less important (and certainly no more important) than what your organization is contributing to people's lives.

We can also try to give everyone a shot at doing work whose potential impact on our future is significant. Making every project summary or status report include a section called "Impact on the Far-off Future" will get everyone's eye on that distant ball.

Memorialize Great Efforts

We can provide opportunities for people's names to be associated with worthy causes. A donation to a hospital in honor of a great effort, combined with a first-class plaque with the names of the people who accomplished it, could stir souls to great accomplishment.

Give Opportunities to Teach

We can give people opportunities to become experts in certain areas and to teach others what they have learned. A required course of training followed by certification in that area of expertise serves both to make the knowledge more sure and to make the effort of attaining it seem more worthwhile. These experts could be listed in an organizational yellow pages or directory so that others will have access to them. Few things give a greater sense of legacy than teaching what you know.

Develop and Honor Mentors

The apprenticeship system was designed to transfer knowledge to younger craftsmen while providing support to the master. But make no mistake: The honor of being master, a mentor, was part of the "pay." Have special recognition and awards for those who mentor passionately, who mentor many, who leave an echo of their presence in many places in the organization.

Intrapreneur

We can structure our organizations so that many or even most of our people can run their own "businesses" within our business. Most people worth their salt were not designed to happily work for an organization or for other people, yet even in highly entrepreneurial societies like the United States, studies show that 90 percent of the workers work for someone else. Just by becoming employees in most organizations, people have lost a piece of something very important about themselves. The other bad news is that this has been lost to the organization as well.

If we are leaders, we want to call our own shots; if we want all of our people to be leaders, we have to let them call their own shots, too. The possibilities of moving up the ladder are very limited today, perhaps more so than ever. We need more ladders—a whole lot more. Or maybe just fewer steps. We have to create multiple "businesses," each with its own "CEO." Every natural work group is a small business waiting to "go public."

Give Them a Voice

We can find some way to give our people a voice today that will be heard many years from now. A time capsule, in which people talk about their work and where they see the organization going in the next decades, could be recorded and played at some set time, say ten or twenty years in the future. If these people are still there to hear what they sounded like, that will be terrific, but just the knowledge that they will be heard again someday will be very satisfying.

We can also let people know that they will be addressing some group five years hence on the topic "passionate projects of the past five years."

Make passion the key criterion for assigning these opportunities. Let people know that fire spreads, and that we will always give a forum to those who have it burning.

Give Them a Vote

If we are honest, we have to admit that many decisions we make about the future are merely educated guesses among competing options. Why not present some of these options to our people in a fair, balanced, and fully informed way and let them tell us where they want to go? We won't do this if we are insecure, or if we really don't have much confidence in the passion, intelligence, or ability of our people. But think of the passion we will see if they are working on an entire direction that they themselves had a key role in setting.

Treat Everybody as if Their Existence Has Value

Everybody out there has a unique life story, which means that everyone out there can make a unique contribution. Who are these people? How did they arrive at who they now are? What untapped power lies within them?

We need to get past people-as-resource, people-as-asset, people-as-skill-set thinking. It isn't wrong so much as it's inadequate. It's like thinking of a priceless antique car as transportation.

When I'm sitting down to hire or evaluate or promote or teach someone, I try to remind myself of the potential of this incredible being who sits before me—for good or harm. And I ask the person, "Unfettered by life's details, what do you want to *do* with yourself? Where do you want to leave your mark? When the show is over, what do we put on your tombstone?"

If there's a match between the person's answers and our organization—if we can offer this person the opportunity to contribute at the level of the reason why she or he is here on this planet—we won't need to be concerned about employee retention and motivation and productivity. No ten ordinary, good "employees" will be able to come close to one so freed to fly.

We don't have to take all these steps, or even any of them. But if we want to build a passionate organization, if we want our people to beat the socks off both the competition and their own past accomplishments, if we want to have our people's need to make a difference work to give us an edge, we'll do all of them, or some version of all of them, and anything else we can think of as well.

Commitment

For people to work in "the zone," to really achieve at high levels, they have to be committed.

They are not likely to be committed to an organization just because it is there, or is big, or has a good reputation. But they will commit to an idea or dream or goal or cause *as it is embodied in an organization*. The organization isn't the thing; the cause is the thing. We have to create our organization with some embedded cause or causes that people can be committed to in a nonrational (not irrational) way.

"Leaders understand very basic truth about human beings," say Warren Bennis and Patricia Ward Biederman. "They know that we long for meaning. Without meaning, *labor is time stolen from us*"[2] (emphasis added). Too many people are planning to begin living when they retire, often because their work has no meaning for them. Their resentment toward us and our organization over a long period of working without meaning cannot be eliminated. It will kill them from the inside out, and it will ensure that only a small part of the excellence that resides in them will ever benefit our organization. As Boris Pasternak said in his novel *Doctor Zhivago*, "Man is born to live and not to prepare to live."

For years, many organizations have construed the payment of wages to mean, "We've laid our money on the line, and basically we own you employees. You're indentured servants—unless we can figure out how to make you slaves." A slightly more enlightened approach saw it as an exchange: "You give us your time and effort, and we will give you wages and benefits." Some reached the next level of thought, which is, "We come to the table as equals. We will develop you and give you opportunities and recognition, and you will use your skills and dedication to make us more successful." Many organizations are light-years away from even *seeing* this level.

But there is more. There is yet another level, which is, "You are making an investment of your time, life, and soul into this organization. We will treat you as we treat our financial investors. Your development will cost us money, which we will treat as an investment rather than a cost. And we won't gripe about it, because your passionate effort is worth more on our measurement scale than we could ever afford to pay you or spend on you."

When we make an investment, our commitment to that investment is only as strong as the returns we are receiving or believe we will receive. In a real way, people who labor for our organization are investing their very lives in our vision. What is their ROI? They are paying a very precious price for their earnings. What is their P/E ratio? Who is making the bigger investment, those who invest their money or those who invest themselves?

It doesn't matter if everyone in the world is or could be committed to our vision, our purpose. It only matters that everyone inside our organization is committed to.

Conclusion

We and our people have an inner need to make a difference. With passion and thought, our organizational pulse can welcome this need and nurture it, and our organizational design can give it form.

If we tap into this need, their commitment and passion will be ours.

Notes

1. As quoted in *HR Focus,* May 1998, p. 8.
2. Warren Bennis and Patricia Ward Biederman, *Organizing Genius: The Secrets of Creative Collaboration* (Reading, Mass.: Addison-Wesley Publishing Company, Inc., 1997), p. 23.

10

Balanced People With Multiple Passions

Those who are skilled in archery bend their bow only when they are preparing to use it; when they do not require it, they allow it to remain unbent, for otherwise it would be unserviceable when the time for using it arrived. So it is with man. If he were to devote himself unceasingly to a dull round of business, without breaking the monotony by cheerful amusements, he would fall imperceptibly into idiocy, or be struck by paralysis. It is the conviction of this truth that leads to the proper division of my time.

—Herodotus, *History of the Persian War*

Our minds need relaxation, and give way
Unless we mix with work a little play.

—Molière, French dramatist

If a man walk in the woods for love of them half of each day, he is in danger of being regarded as a loafer, but if he spends his whole day as a speculator, shearing off those woods and making earth bald before her time, he is esteemed an industrious and enterprising citizen. As if a town had no interest in its forests but to cut them down!

—Henry David Thoreau, *Life Without Principle*

Let's face it: Many leaders and organizations see the "outside" passions of their people as irrelevant (or, worse, as a distraction from their work efforts). They want "monomaniacs with a mission," to use a current phrase that catches half the truth.

This approach loses big for two reasons.

First, it misses the contagious nature of passion. People who have come to life in one area usually are more effective in other areas of their lives. We should be happy when our people are excited about politics, their local communities, their churches, going back to school, or building their own house. Their enthusiasm tells us that there is still a spark inside those people, still some life, still something into which we can tap. God help the person who no longer finds anything interesting.

It is all too easy to feel threatened by these outside passions and succumb to the fear that they will distract our people from their work. The problem with this is that we are thinking of people in terms of their limitations—they have only so much energy, and outside interests will just use it up. The solution is to think of people in terms of their possibilities—they're using only a small portion of their passion, and outside interests are just fuel for the fire. It means that as leaders, we have to help our people become "larger," rather than simply hogging the smallness that we perceive to be there.

Our experience tells us that the busiest, most energetic people are usually the ones who are the most willing and (somehow) able to take on new missions and assignments. To be sure, they can overcommit, but even then they will often find the energy and creativity to make it all happen. Lethargic people, on the other hand, will find it hard to do anything new, even if their evenings and weekends are basically free.

What's the difference between the two?

It isn't really a matter of time, or even of the number of projects or activities. It is a matter of *desire*. Of *enthusiasm*. Of *zest*. Of *passion*. The energetic approach to life is expansive: Energy feeds energy, passion builds passion. I want people working for me who are passionate about everything they do. And I want people who are passionate about more than just one thing.

Second, because of its orientation toward compartmentalizing and fragmenting, the distraction view of outside interests also eliminates the opportunities for bisociation and synergy between and among various aspects of our lives.

We need multidimensional people who can tie their passions together. We need people who read widely and outside of their field. We need people who care about interesting and even odd issues. We need people who see the world as a whole, not just bits and pieces. We need people who are smart enough to do a complex job and wise enough to stop when they see its negative implications.

The best new ideas seldom come as an extrapolation of the current approach, and yet most employees are expected to be knowledgeable only about that approach, only about what's in their job description. Instead, the best new ideas usually come in the cracks, in combinations of ideas from widely divergent fields of knowledge (which are all part of some coherent whole).

For example, some entrepreneurs saw busy people traveling and running between meetings. They watched these movers and shakers conducting major business on their cellular and digital phones. They observed the rise of e-mail and general use of the internet, and, at the same time, the rise of information overload. They were aware of advances in speech technology (voice recognition). The result of these social and technical observations? The concept of seamlessly accessible information. Now you can access your e-mail on your cell phone and give verbal instructions that are converted to e-mail messages. A whole new business has arisen, synthesized out of separate, but—to those paying attention—deeply interrelated concepts.

We need to take the time to find out what people are passionate about. It is fairly easy to determine what their skills are. With more probing, we can find out how they think. A yet deeper probe can highlight their values and convictions. But only time, combined with the right questions, can help us see where the fire is. And if the fire is in a field or area unrelated on the surface to the job we have for them, but the core of the job requires that very sort of fire, would we not be wise to reassign them based on their passion?

In hiring and assigning people, we should let their hearts overrule our heads—because while they're on the job, their hearts will surely overrule their heads.

Monomaniacs with a mission can be pretty scary people. I don't want them working for me. But "polymaniacs with missions" are a whole other story. They have a number of projects going on various issues that command their attention; they care passionately about all of them; when they need to focus on one of them, get out of the way; and they know when enough is enough.

This also ties in with another debate: Do people need specialized skills or general skills? Yes. This is another false trade-off. People need specialized skills in a few areas where they can be maniacs now,

and general skills so that they will know where to be maniacs later—
and also so that they can be balanced polymaniacs.

The Balanced Polymaniac

A zealot is "One who is zealous, especially excessively so. . . . A fa-
natically committed person."[1] We need people who can take us over
the top. But we don't need the extreme version, the zealot—someone
who *is* over the top.

Zealots go beyond passion, which is needed to accomplish any
great goal. The philosopher George Santayana once noted, "Fanati-
cism consists in redoubling your effort when you have forgotten your
aim." And there's no use trying to correct them. "No good can ever
result from any attempt to set one of these fiery zealots to rights, either in fact or principle," warned Thomas Jefferson. "They are determined as to the facts they will believe, and the opinions on which
they will act. Get by them, therefore, as you would by an angry bull;
it is not for a man of sense to dispute the road with such an animal."

The quickest way to identify zealots is to count the number of
issues about which they are passionate. Zealots are focused on one
goal; all else pales and disappears. Even if the goal is a good one, it
too easily degenerates into a crusade that kills people if they won't
convert. To the zealot, the goal seems bigger and more important
than it really is. It demands efforts that are not commensurate with
the ends. Everyone who is not a zealot on that cause is deemed a
cretin, a fool, or worse. It makes me very nervous when I hear that
someone has only one serious interest. "Nothing is more dangerous
than an idea when it is the only one you have," said French essayist
Émile Chartier.

We cannot afford to have zealots working for us or around us.
Maniacal, overly demanding people, people who insist that their
mission be paramount, will turn other people off. We need people's
willing involvement, not what we can demand from them or beat
out of them.

But we need to be careful. Some who appear to be zealots are really passionate people with a major issue or a current focus:

• *Theodore Roosevelt* was a zealous progressive and populist—
but he also wrote thirty-six books (more, I m afraid, than some presi-

dents have read); read up to three books a day; was a noted conservationist, environmentalist, and naturalist; won the Nobel Peace Prize; and *after* he was president of the United States, explored a river in Brazil in a journey that compared well with the Lewis and Clark expedition (the river was named after him).

• *Thomas Jefferson* was a zealous freedom fighter (the good kind, from principle and not over the bodies of children)—but he also built a 10,000-volume library (which became the Library of Congress), founded the University of Virginia, wrote correspondence and other writings that fill sixty volumes, and was a tireless inventor and scientist.

• *Peter Drucker* has been the leading thinker on leadership and organizations for half a century—but he has also written extensively on economics, politics, and society; penned two novels; and become a mini-expert on fields as diverse as Japanese art.

• *William Gladstone* spent sixty-three years in the British House of Commons, served twenty-seven years in the cabinet, and was prime minister four times—but he also read 20,000 books, was a classical scholar, and wrote on a wide range of topics.[2]

• *Susan B. Anthony* was called the hard-charging "Napoleon" of the American women's suffrage movement in the nineteenth century—but she was also an abolitionist, an educational reformer, a labor activist, a temperance worker, the publisher of a newspaper, and an author.

• *Max DePree* was the successful and beloved CEO of Herman Miller, Inc.—but he also became a respected leadership consultant, a best-selling author (*Leadership Is an Art* and *Leadership Jazz*), and a vulnerable human being who can "think out loud" on the key questions of life (as, for example, in his moving book about the premature birth of his granddaughter).[3]

We need this kind of passion in our organization—people who are utterly devoted to a number of visions, missions, plans, goals, projects, or processes. Getting anything done in life, against the massive opposing forces and the insidious power of inertia, is extremely difficult—much more difficult than the motivational gurus would have us believe. It can take mighty, draining, relentless power to make even small changes. Only a person full of passion can get the job done.

Why?

• Most people won't honestly care about even very worthwhile ideas. It is unrealistic to expect them to. We have to have "surrogate carers," people who care enough about that particular idea for all of us.

• Most people don't want to change and don't want change, period. "People like to talk about change, which makes them feel good, rather than actually change, which makes them feel bad."[4] They want a little bit of security in a pretty dynamic and unfathomable world. We have to sell change, even as we recognize that change can't really be sold. It can only be accommodated (and we thrive) or resisted (and we die). Passionate people understand that change is at the core of future success. Not only are they willing to change, they love change, welcome it, will fight and even die for it.

• People who may never have an idea of their own for which to fight will spend their energies trying to kill a new idea or direction. The only "synergy" they know is the power to collaborate with other killers to stop the passionate person. These forces for ill should not be underestimated. It will take a champion to knock them down.

• Life takes its toll. We have to start with a deep reservoir of passion if we are going to have anything left to finish the effort.

• Only a passionate person will do the homework necessary to make sure that the idea is fully developed and implemented. Almost everything in life is difficult to some degree. The "give up" factor is high for all of us. Passionate people won't accept it. Their non-rational, positive passion drives them to be excellent in the rational development of their ideas.

We are suggesting an organization full of passionate people. But they must be balanced. "A fanatic is one who can't change his mind and won't change the subject," said Winston Churchill. Our people cannot be fanatics. This means that they cannot focus on their idea to the exclusion of all other responsibilities. It means that they cannot pursue their idea when it has been clearly shown that it cannot be achieved, at least with the available resources, technology, etc. It means that they cannot pursue their idea to the detriment of other critical projects that have their own champions. And it means that they need to learn how to compromise.

Compromise. I have to admit that I really hate the word, or at least its connotations. It implies a giving up, perhaps even of our principles. The dictionary defines it as, "A settlement of differences in which each side makes concessions."[5] A compromise that insists on a sacrifice of values that amounts to compromising our principles, is a bad bargain indeed. This kind of compromise is a purchased peace, an appeasement, rather than the peace that comes from advancing toward a dream.

But the concessions don't have to be of principle. They can be much more creative than that. The second definition of *compromise* is, "Something that combines qualities or elements of different things." The word itself comes from a root that means "to promise mutually."

People with positive passion need to learn how to combine qualities or elements of different things, to promise mutually. They need to know that champions of other causes aren't obstacles to their own visions (at least not at first), but rather represent the opportunity for both of their dreams to grow bigger. The root of the word implies how this is to be done: "to promise mutually." I agree to do this if you agree to do that; I agree to give this up if you will lay that aside.

To aid these people in the process of compromising, we can help them explore the answers to the following questions: What issues or causes or goals would you fight to the organizational death for? What issues or causes or goals would you permit to go to the back burner for a time, but never be taken off the stove? Which issues do you think will still be important to you in ten or twenty years? What is important to you that you are not spending time on now but plan to devote yourself to later?

We will further explore the negative passion generated by fanatics in Chapter 15. Suffice it to say here that single-issue zealots are a bad bet. If someone is on a crusade, make sure she's got some other passions in her saddlebags.

Balance Between People

We need to have individual polymaniacs who balance multiple passions in their own lives. And we need to have polymaniacs who can balance one another, at least at their points of passion.

Jerry Hirshberg speaks about "hiring in divergent pairs."[6] The divergence is not just in skills or experience, but primarily in interests and enthusiasms. We need to think about how a new hire's passion points can be balanced by, offset by, and enhanced by the passion points of current and possible future members of the organization.

This is contrary to the rational approach, which tells us that "birds of a feather flock together" and "great minds think alike." The truth is that small minds flock together and think alike. If our people are alike rather than contrasting, they can easily reaffirm one another's weaknesses and stupid ideas. It takes a different mindset to be able to say, "I know we've done it this way for years, and I know you all think this plan is terrific, but it has no bearing on what our customers really want—even though they aren't yet able to articulate those wants."

This means that we as leaders need to become more comfortable with conflict and tension and less comfortable with comfort. Leaders of large organizations (and even many small organizations) rarely hear the truth or the passion because it has all been filtered out along the way. People below us want to "present a united front." We hear the recommendation, but not the war that led up to it or the dissenters that may be right.

When we hear a passionless, reasonable, rational presentation, we need to be discontented, even disturbed. We need to start asking and probing and digging until we find out where the passion is—whether it is for or against. We need to prefer the polymaniac who is missing a few facts to the rational presenter who is missing the fire, who cares only about not making a mistake or getting criticized.

Balance Between Work and the Rest of Life

People today want, need, and demand balance in their lives. According to the 1998 *American Graduate Survey,* the overwhelming top priority of new graduates entering the workforce is to balance personal life and career.[7] In a survey of over 10,000 workers in thirteen countries, "Across the major geographic regions, respondents selected 'balance the needs of work and family or personal life' as either the most or second-most important attribute in a job."[8]

People no longer want to sacrifice their families and friends and avocations and hobbies and charitable work for "the good of the organization." They wonder what kind of carnivorous organization would demand this kind of sacrifice in the first place. "Perpetual devotion to what a man calls his business is only to be sustained by perpetual neglect of many other things," reminds British author Robert Louis Stevenson.

There is a huge difference between people's choosing to make a sacrifice and an organization's demanding a sacrifice from them. If people are passionate about what they do, they will constantly make their own trade-offs—they will be late for dinner tonight but go in late Friday so that they can have breakfast with the kids. They will know it isn't either/or, it's both/and.

Many writers and thinkers have tried to set up priority schemes. These can read "God, country, king" or "family, church, work," but they all fall down in practice because we can't divide our lives up so neatly. Can we really *always* put family activities over everything related to our work? No way. I might spend the whole day today with my child, tomorrow on my job, and the next day on my own spiritual development. Or, more likely, all three days may be a mix, in varying proportions, of all of these areas. One-time prioritization is rational, but it isn't real.

Life, from one perspective, is a series of trade-offs. Passionate people will make the sacrifices to do what they are passionate about. We've just got to make sure that one of their primary passions is our vision and related goals.

This is very different from demanding sacrifices. Even if I want to do something passionately, if you insist on it, my passion level will decline. Speeches about "making sacrifices" are almost always counterproductive. The only time they seem to work is when everyone already sees the need for sacrifice and is passionate about winning, as when Winston Churchill called on the British people to sacrifice to stand alone against the juggernaut of Nazi Germany.

What people end up doing is dividing their lives into a "do what I have to now" portion and a "do what I want to then" portion. "It's inevitable that they split their lives because corporations are so greedy about time," says British writer and philosopher Charles Handy.[9] It is much better to build flexibility into our rules so that people can blend and flow rather than divide and compartmentalize. We can blur the lines between work and the rest of life—not in the usual way by expecting people to take work home, but by creating opportunities for people to bring the rest of their lives into work. This could include bringing families to open houses and internal trade fairs, involving families and friends in surveys and opinion polls (e.g. "What do you think of our new logo?"), or having a hobby display and discussion day.

We can help ourselves by thinking of our people practically (if not legally) as independent contractors who control how they set their priorities and divide up their time. This means:

- They are on their own to develop skills, shift emphases, and find out what their "customer" (the organization) needs.
- The organization "owns" the customers and assigns the "contract" (the work), and the contractors own their "business" (career), skills, and knowledge.
- We understand that it isn't bad that they are independent—often independent contractors must be better than employees to keep the work coming.

Balance Between Work and Rest

We want people who know both how to fly and when to come in for a landing.

Any experienced farmer knows that land has to be rested as well as worked if it is to be productive and enduring. Any experienced manufacturing manager or engineer knows that equipment has to be taken out of service for preventive maintenance if it is to be productive and enduring. Any experienced parent knows that small children have to have naps if they are to be productive (learn and grow) and enduring (make it through childhood alive).

There are cycles to all aspects of our lives, and we ignore them at our peril. Leaders who are absolutely brilliant, who know all about the need for fallow ground and preventive maintenance and naps for small children, can completely miss the need for rest for their most important asset.

People in many organizations are terrified at the prospect of someone in management seeing them take a break, chat with a friend, skim through a magazine, or stare out a window. We can feel guilty about not coming in on a weekend, and feel obligated to give a number where we can be reached on vacation. Because rest is bad. Rest is stealing. Rest is evil.

On the contrary, rest is good, rest is value-enhancing, rest is sublime. It's *not* resting that's bad. "The American Institute of Stress reports that 66 percent of all visits to primary-care physicians are for stress-related disorders. Stress is a heavy contributor to heart disease, cancer, respiratory distress, and many other life-threatening illnesses. Job-related stress costs American industry between $100 and $300 billion a year in absenteeism, poor service, lost productivity, mistakes and accidents, medical insurance, and workers' compensation claims."[10]

It all comes out in the end. If we work seven days a week without a break, the time lost to recharging will have to be paid back sometime. If we need, say, one day's rest in seven and never take it, will those fifty-two days a year, compounded over decades, all be deducted at the end of a shortened, worn-out life? "Too much work kills a man just as effectively as too much assorted vice or too much drink," wrote British author Rudyard Kipling. Rest isn't a throwaway; it's a positively brilliant competitive advantage.

A true sabbatical can recharge our people at the core (as well as be an incredible retention tool). Some organizations have a formal sabbatical program, and more will look into this in the near future. At Information Management Consultants in McClean, Virginia, employees earn a twelve-week paid sabbatical for every seven years of service. The only restriction is that they must return the pay if they take another job in the following twelve months. "People really appreciate this," Chairman Sudhakar Shenoy told me. "They come back fresh and ready to contribute." A sabbatical isn't a costly gift; it is a very intelligent investment in passion.

We also need to "rest" from projects that are stymied. "Work has its own gravitational field, and the intervention of skilled leadership can help in occasionally pulling away from it. This, however, is a counterintuitive move, one that can appear (and even feel) irresponsible and inefficient to those not directly involved."[11] It takes great knowledge and wisdom to know when to lay something aside for its long-term advantage, to recharge so that we can be even more effective.

When we see people take a break, we need to think, "Great! They're recharging!" not, "What slackers." When we see them chatting, we need to think, "Terrific! They're actually communicating!" not, "Bunch of idlers." When we see them skim a magazine, we need to think, "They're absorbing new stuff," not, "Wastrel!" And when we see them staring out the window, we need to think, "I'm so pleased that they're thinking," not, "Get your mind back on your work."

Opening the Floodgates of Whole-Life Passion

In this area of balance, there are some techniques that organizations can employ to open the floodgates of whole-life passion.

• We can recognize that we are leading whole people. They may be fragmented and even in personal disarray, but they are still complex beings with multiple areas of life to be lived and accounted for.

• We can believe that passion, as long as it is constructive, is valuable wherever it is found. It is contagious. It is a force that we can tap into to accomplish organizational goals.

• We can explore, rather than suppress, people's passions. "The goal is balance, not emotional suppression: Every feeling has its value and significance. A life without passion would be a dull wasteland of neutrality, cut off and isolated from the richness of life itself."[12] Effective leaders understand and validate the feelings and emotions of their followers. Our tendency in the midst of a busy life is to say, "Don't bother me with your ideas, even though you are excited about them." But we can't relate to others as half people and then expect whole effort from them.

• We can choose to hire balanced polymaniacs—balanced within themselves and balanced with others in the organization.

• We can take steps to ensure that our people have the opportunity to explore the best of who they are inside, the opportunity to live a full life.

• We can insist on the need for rest as a productive tool, and the need to step away for a while from even a critical project to get perspective.

After centuries of advanced economic life, the time has come to lay aside all of the demeaning ideas about people—as tools, as cogs, as assets, as resources—and treat them instead with the dignity and respect befitting such complex, amazing, and often noble beings.

Conclusion

We want the fire.
But we've got to take it all.

Notes

1. *The American Heritage Dictionary of the English Language, Third Edition.* (Boston: Houghton Mifflin Company, 1996).

2. See Roy Jenkins, *Gladstone: A Biography* (New York: Random House, 1997).
3. Max DePree, *Dear Zoe: Letters to My Grandchild on the Wonder of Life* (Grand Rapids, Mich.: Wm. B. Eerdmans Publishing Co., 1996).
4. Laura Lucas, teacher, writer, and director.
5. *The American Heritage Dictionary of the English Language, Third Edition* (Boston: Houghton Mifflin Company, 1996).
6. See Jerry Hirshberg, *The Creative Priority: Driving Innovative Business in the Real World* (New York: HarperBusiness, 1998).
7. As reported in "New Recruits Say 'Let's Get a Life!' " *Management Review,* July/August 1998, p. 7.
8. "Workers Everywhere Want the Same Things," *Global Workforce,* November 1998, p. 8.
9. As quoted in *Management Review,* June 1998, p. 53.
10. John E. Newman, *How to Stay Cool, Calm & Collected When the Pressure's On: A Stress-Control Plan for Businesspeople* (New York: AMACOM, 1992), p. 14.
11. Hirshberg, p. 179.
12. Daniel Goleman, *Emotional Intelligence* (New York: Bantam Books, 1995), p. 56.

PART III

THE PASSIONATE ORGANIZATION

In the previous section, we looked at how organizations can tap into the passions that are latent in their employees, to the benefit of both parties.

In this section, we will look at the attitudes and practices of passionate organizations. We will discuss how to hire and promote passionate people, the starting point for success. We will then review some concepts that will allow us to direct these people's passions so that everyone is working toward the same goal, the good of all stakeholders. We will discuss how to stoke the fire in those whose passion is waning, and how to recognize and respond to those whose only passion is to further themselves or to hurt the organization.

We will conclude by examining three obstacles—the concept of management, the fear of failure and mistakes, and clinging to the status quo—that leaders must destroy if their organizations are to be truly passionate.

11

Pick and Prepare Passionate People

Do not hire a man who does your work for money, but him who does it for love of it.

—Henry David Thoreau, *Life Without Principle*

I want to get rid of the living dead. I can't stand going into factories and businesses and seeing those faceless people standing around. They don't look healthy and they don't act healthy, and they're a big problem for corporate America. I'm talking about people who are there because it's a job, whose attitude is, "I have to be here, but I don't have to like it." . . . What have we done to create these types of environments? We should be able to tell this person, "It's your obligation to be happy. Find somewhere to be happy."

—Jack Stack, *The Great Game of Business*

We're not money hungry. We're good at what we do, and we enjoy what we're doing. We feel that we're making a big difference in people's lives, and that turns us on.

—Carlton Caldwell, president, Caldwell Laboratories, *Best of Business Quarterly*

Although passion and fire can't be controlled, they can be discerned and selected and nurtured. We can find the right people for the right missions, and then watch as they begin to move passionately in directions we could never have imagined.

The Passion Match

Although it presents its own challenges, hiring people with particular skills and aptitudes is a relatively easy process.

We can get a fairly good understanding of these "head" parameters through job history, evaluation of past performance both in school and on the job, and standard tests. If someone has an aptitude, for example, for math, it shouldn't be too difficult to find that out. Has this person worked in jobs that required math skills? Did he do well in those jobs? Did he consistently score well in his math courses? How did he come out on our math tests? Expertise should rise to the top. In any kind of intensive screening process, skills and aptitudes should become obvious.

What is not so obvious, however, is whether the person *enjoys* exercising those skills, *cares* about that sort of work, and is *passionate* about the directions that those aptitudes imply. "One of the most common mistakes we've seen people make in managing their careers is basing their initial (and subsequent) career choices on their aptitudes rather than on their interests."[1] This is the fatal deficiency of most career planning.

And this is the ultimate failing of surveys that attempt to discern the levels of satisfaction of people in the workplace. Because levels of satisfaction are often scored "high,"[2] the assumption is made that the person is in the right type of work. Questions then revolve around working *conditions* (for example, communication with the boss, friends at work, having the opportunity to make decisions) rather than the *fit*, the appropriateness of the work itself. The surveys may be a good barometer of the fit of the workplace for actual human beings, but not of the fit of the human beings for their actual workplaces.

Surely, people will enjoy a progressive, enlightened workplace more than an oppressive one, and oppressors are at least hiding better than they used to. But if I am not passionate about the actual work I am doing, or at least about a substantial portion of it, I will not—and cannot—give it my best, perform at the highest levels of which I am capable, and be creative—at least, not for very long. The will to do it won't hold up over the long run.

In advanced economies, at least, we should be far past the "warm body" theory that says, "Just get someone in here to fill that position." (Although low employment rates can cause us to forget what we've learned.) But we should also be advancing past the rational approach that says, "Let's get someone in here with the skills, or at least the aptitudes, to do this job." The rational approach is certainly far better than the warm body approach. In slower and more stable times, it was probably enough to ensure at least some measure of organizational and personal success in most cases (although the loss of individual potential, achievement, and satisfaction should not be underestimated).

But we should take a deeper, richer, better approach: hiring on the passion scale. As we've already discussed, people who are passionate about their work *because they love it* will perform at the highest possible personal level, be more creative, be more committed, be readier to sacrifice, and be less likely to look for greener pastures. The difference between this kind of employee and the rational fit may be immeasurable. Furthermore, organizations staffed with these passionate people will operate at the highest possible levels, be more creative, be more focused, have more tenacity, and build more momentum over time.

We're not saying that the rational-fit approach is bad. We are simply saying that it is no longer enough to put us at the head of the pack. And, if there is a passionate organization or two in our industry, it may not even be enough to enable us to survive.

How Do We Hire for Passion?

Hiring for passion does take a plan.

In Chapter 6, we discussed some general clues to use and questions to ask in order to discern the presence of passion. With regard to the particular area of hiring, I especially look at six key areas in which prospective employees have to score high.

1. *Passion for life.* Are they excited about being alive? Does it come across in their life narratives? Or are they complainers or victims? Sooner or later, life gives everyone a beating. What was their beating? How have they responded? Has it taken the life, the passion, out of them? Or has it caused them to redouble their efforts?

2. *Passion for the vision.* Do they care about our picture of a desirable future? Does it excite them? Do they even know what it is? Do they feel that our purpose, our reason for existence, is noble? Or does it strike them as mundane or boring?

3. *Passion for the values.* Do our core organizational values resonate with them? Which ones really fire them up? Which ones bring a yawn? Do they disagree with any of them? Which ones would they be willing

to spend themselves on? Or sacrifice themselves over? Or ignore? Or violate?

4. *Passion for the work.* Do they have a visceral reaction to the position we are offering? Do they think it worthy of their best efforts? Will they on their own come in early and work late, and think about it on weekends and vacations, because it is just so damn exciting?

5. *Passion for variety.* Are they balanced polymaniacs? Are they curious about a lot of stuff? Are they excited about new ideas? Or do they nod and say, "I see, I see?"

6. *Passion for others.* Do they really care about other people? Do they place a high value on relationships and connection, not as a networking tool but as a centerpiece of organizational life? Or do they have a bit of arrogance, self-centeredness, even narcissism? A fire is smothered when it is turned in on itself. We need people who have a passion for other people.

7. *Passion for leaving a mark.* What sort of impact do they want to have on the organization? How do they intend to go about doing it? Do they intend to make this a stopover or a show-stopper?

How do we test for the above? We have to be creative. We have to listen for their tone and watch their body language. We have to let them talk with a number of our passionate people—hourly and salaried—and have our people rate them on the passion scale. (A thorough list of questions our people can use was given in Chapter 6.) If everyone who interviews an applicant isn't passionate about the person, it's time to move on. Psychological testing and evaluation can help, if they get past superficial generalizations and really get down to drivers.

This kind of matching takes time. The alternative is to rush through hiring to "save time," and then spend vast amounts of time trying to keep the person from wrecking the organization's passion. If we hire fast, we'll suffer slow.

The criticality of this process is magnified when a new operation is being built from scratch. "It cost us almost $1 million to get our first fifty-four employees," Karl Eberle, vice president and general manager of Harley-Davidson's flagship Kansas City plant, told me. "We spend a lot of time and effort making sure the selection process is right. Salary and hourly alike, there is just a lot of effort put into it." And Harley (Kansas City) gives everyone two weeks of training before it lets them on the floor.

Overall, "the single best predictor of overall excellence was a company's ability to attract, motivate, and retain talented people."[3] If we hire for passion, they will come, they will stay, and they will motivate themselves.

Build a Farm Team

We can't rely on free agents and walk-ons if we want to build a dynasty of passion. We've got to have a farm team.

True partnerships with schools, starting in high school (or maybe even earlier), are the key. The artificial wall between schooling and work, never a brilliant idea, has become a major liability, both to organizations and to individuals.

One innovative and highly successful program is the Community Learning Program (CLP) at McCluer North High School in St. Louis County, Missouri, a school that is on the *Redbook* list of "America's Best Schools" and is nationally recognized for excellence by the U.S. Department of Education. "There are a number of things that differentiate the CLP from other school-business partnership programs," John Reidy, a CLP instructor and coordinator for many years, told me. "First, we attempt to match individual students with the career that really interests them. Second, we have a wide range of offerings for career exploration—if students are interested in something, we find a good organization that will give them real experience. And third, students may not be paid for their experience, so we can get them into programs, observations, and learning activities for which a lot of organizations would be unwilling or unable to pay."

How does it work? Four days a week, students go to their work sites half the day and take classes the other half. On the fifth day, students have a "day in" with their CLP instructor and other CLP students to review and add to their experiences. CLP instructors visit students at their work sites several times a semester to evaluate and review their activities and connect with the sponsors.

Learning includes observation; career "shadowing"; projects, reading, and research assigned by the sponsor; and, where possible, hands-on participation. "Students get to see where their interests really are," says Reidy. The placement process is thorough and demanding. Students have to take the responsibility for getting themselves to their work sites. They are required to write daily in a journal, maintain a time log, and put together a semester project on their chosen field.

"They also get to see, early on and at a small investment, what they *aren't* interested in," Reidy told me. "Many of these students have said how grateful they are that the program kept them from making a big mistake in pursuing a career that would have left them flat."

We're not talking about typical "tech school" types of assignments. Students have been placed in such areas as archaeology, television and radio, law and law enforcement, nursing, operating rooms, cardiology, hotel management, public relations, wildlife management, architecture, teaching, special education, and meteorology.

The list of sponsors is impressive. Organizations include American Airlines, McDonnell Douglas (now Boeing), Emerson Electric, the St. Louis Zoo, KMOX Radio, KSD-TV, St. John's Hospital, the Florissant and Hazelwood Police Departments, St. Louis County Juvenile Court, the St. Louis Health Department, the St. Louis Airport Traffic Control Tower, and the Washington University Medical School.

How successful is the program? "We've been doing this since 1971," Reidy, who is obviously passionate about the CLP, told me. "In our last extensive survey of CLP graduates, 92 percent said it was their most rewarding high school experience, and 95 percent said it helped them make good career decisions." The benefit to the sponsors? "They get excellent community awareness, and many of these students, if the match is good, end up going to work for the sponsor."

There is simply no reason why this type of program couldn't work in community colleges and other colleges and universities. Why not find out, as early as possible and at the smallest personal cost, where students' passions are? Why don't all schools have programs like this? Why wouldn't we start asking them about the possibilities and helping get them off the ground?

This is just one example of "farm team" thinking. At the core, this thinking says: Let's find people early in their lives and careers who align with our vision and values. Let's develop strong up-through-the-ranks policies to ensure that we develop and promote people based on their living out and *enhancing* the vision and values. And let's make sure that our people are very diverse in every other way, so that our strong, unifying vision and values don't degenerate into rigidity and stagnation.

The opportunity to make passion matches is there, and we can make this career thing better for all concerned.

Let Them Learn by Passion

Traditional training focuses on telling, showing, and doing. It assumes that if people know, they will do.

Training in the passionate organization will still give people the instruction (how to do it), but will spend an equal amount of time exposing and building their inspiration (desire and energy to do it). Assuming that people have sparks inside themselves, learning can fan these sparks into a roaring fire. This recognizes the reality that before people implement what they have learned, they have to "work it in." They have to be able to understand why it's important. They have to be able to challenge it, question it, wrestle with it, and make it their own. They have to really see how the learning ties in with, and enhances, their passion.

Learning in the passionate organization will take on more of a "buffet" feel, with people selecting and implementing their own developmental avenues from a broad selection of possibilities. The range of learning offered will itself be widened considerably as those responsible come to realize that all knowledge is interdependent and that useful learning can come from unlikely sources.

We can try to offer learning that simply can't be gotten anywhere else. Why not set our targets high? Why not have learning opportunities that stretch and amaze us rather than make us yawn? We can get standard training from a wide variety of sources, so there's no reason to duplicate it. Let's place our chips on knock-your-socks-off learning experiences.

One important issue becomes, "How will we provide all this learning?" A lot of organizations simply say, "We'll do it." As of this writing, Saturn, Zytec, Shell (Houston), Wainwright Industries, Interface, and Kingston Technology average over a hundred hours of training per employee per year, while LL Bean, Lands End, Texas Instruments, Cisco Systems, and Corning average eighty hours or more.

An approach that can work in many organizations is "earning learning." If people or groups finish their work or hit their targets early, they can spend their remaining time in development activity. It's true that if we learn more, we'll earn more. Why not reverse the formula and earn more to learn more—earning time and opportunity?

The key question in all this becomes, "What do you want to learn?" even before "What do you need to learn?" We need to maximize the time our people spend in learning that excites them. We shouldn't have to motivate people to learn. What they are *learning* should motivate them to learn. All learning should cause feedback. They have learned it. Now what? Do they really love it? Do they have a hunger to learn even more about it?

We can let our people establish a program for themselves, and reward and recognize them for achieving the end goal or milestones along the way. But again, the rewards and recognition aren't the thing; the learning is the thing. If they love it, that's enough.

The same principle is true for learning in general. If I don't like the subject, it is torturous to make myself get into it. If I'm really interested in it, I'll squeeze in reading or studying about it whenever possible. Through grade school, perhaps, we need to teach children basic skills in all subjects, even those in which they have little interest. Even there, though, giving them more of what they are interested in and getting out of the "commodity" mentality would probably reap a good passion harvest. But certainly after grade school we should provide as many opportunities as possible for students to focus on areas of personal interest.

The same principle is true in the workplace. We need to tailor our learning to the individual, not make the individual fit the program. By the time people are in high school, their strengths and weaknesses are becoming clear. Why focus on weaknesses rather than strengths? Let's feed the strengths and starve the weaknesses. Let's learn where we are strong—where our passions lie.

Learning by Teaching

Few things cause us to learn more than the need to share what we know with others.

There is no question that we need the teaching organization, made up of teachers who are passionate about their subjects, teaching others who are passionate about the same subjects. Whereas the learning organization has largely been a rational model, the teaching organization is a passionate model. We can structure it to accumulate knowledge, and to disseminate this knowledge to some degree. But we have to encourage teachers who are passionate to turn their knowledge into wisdom and share it enthusiastically with others.

The learning organization's tools are structures to accumulate information and knowledge. The teaching organization's tools are passion and mentors. People have knowledge and wisdom about a topic that they care about deeply. It's in their heads and hearts. Who better to pass it on?

The alternative to dry, programmatic training functions is an organization full of fire, and full of fiery teachers.

Evaluating Passion

Once people are part of our organization, a big part of our ongoing evaluation needs to be on their level of passion.

Are they still excited about the organization and their role in it? Do they have a way to correct the organization if it is going in a bad direction? Can they at least make a big non-career-limiting fuss? Are they enthusiastic about the changes going on around them and the opportunities to exploit those changes?

And what are we doing to squelch their passion? What are *they* doing to squelch their passion? The passionate organization cannot exist if it has very many dispassionate people. They have to be reignited or removed.

Although our ability and desire to be passionate come from choices we have made along the way, the level of passion we feel at any point in time will vary. It will ebb and flow from day to day, month to month, year to year, assignment to assignment, project to project. This means that the evaluation has to occur at two levels: the base level of passion about life and vision and values, and the current level of passion about the work and the relationships.

To evaluate life passion, we're going to have to break one of the cardinal rules of human resources: We're going to have to be aware of, and concerned about, our people's whole lives. Are they happy with where they are going? Do they like who they are and who they are becoming? Do they feel like they are progressing at a good pace toward a valuable goal? Have they examined their lives? People don't want us probing around in all of their issues and dirty laundry, but we do need to make a holistic evaluation.

And how do they really feel about our vision? Does it stir their souls? Ask them to prove it, to tell you how in specific detail. Have they become cynical about our ability to achieve the vision? Cynicism is the death of passion, at least the constructive kind. We aren't trying to get buy-in. We're trying to find out if they have already bought in, or even if they can.

Do they feel kinship with our stated values? Are they living them out in a passionate way? Can their followers see the values in action in their lives? Which ones strike the deepest chords? We can't force these values to ring true. But we can make them known and then listen for the ring.

And how do they feel about their current work? All work has drudgery, but are they excited about 90 percent of what they are doing, and 100 percent of the value they are adding? Are they changing the nature of the job or assignment, or are they merely caretaking? Have they redesigned their work to keep themselves fresh and excited? Have they come up with a substantial number of creative and new ideas? Creativity follows passion. An absence of creativity probably indicates an absence of passion.

Are they enthusiastic about their working relationships? Are they feeling nurtured by those who are teaching them and by those whom they are teaching? How do they feel about the level of passion in the group? Are they adding to it or taking away from it? We need to evaluate them not just on their own personal passion, but on what they do to nurture (or kill) the passion of others.

We need to be aware that as people go through their own personal changes and life transitions, a good match can turn sour. Organizational changes can also affect the match. There is an ongoing need for realignment. Matching is a process, not an event.

Ultimately, workforce alignment comes down to one critical issue: whether the employee's personal vision, values, and interests align with the organization's vision, values, and interests. This is true whether we're talking about new hires, candidates for promotion, people on a career path, or assignments of people to a job, project, or team. If there is no match, there can be no passion.

But if there *is* a match, nothing can stop the fire.

Conclusion

Hire, assign, and promote for passion, and make passion the foundation of your learning and teaching.

Push all other criteria to the back burner.

Notes

1. James Waldrop and Timothy Butler, "Finding the Job You *Should* Want," *Fortune,* March 2, 1998, pp. 211–214.
2. See, for example, Jeffrey L. Seglin, "Americans at Work," *Inc.,* June 1998, pp. 91–94. Although general satisfaction scores were fairly high, the author noted that "just about half of survey respondents said they'd choose a different line of work if they had the chance to start over."
3. "What Makes a Company Great?" *Fortune,* October 26, 1998, p. 218.

12

Encase Passion in Vision and Mutual Trust

A man to carry on a successful business must have imagination. He must see things in a vision, a dream of the whole thing.

—Charles M. Schwab, first president of U.S. Steel

Many of the great strategies are simply great visions. And great visions can be a lot more inspirational and effective than the most carefully constructed plan.

—Henry Mintzberg, Canadian author

The passions are the only orators which always persuade.

—François, duc de La Rochefoucauld, *Sentences et Maximes Morales*

Debra Benton, in a recent issue of *Management Review*, says that we need a leader who is "passionate . . . who understands the need to be melodramatic—to rally people and show passion."

This is true, but insufficient, for success in the coming years.

We need *everyone* to be passionate, not just our designated leaders. To be sure, the passion of formal leaders is critical—it guides, it lives out an example, it exhorts. But it isn't enough. The formal leader can't always be there. The passion has to be built into the mechanisms, into the structures, and deeply into the culture.

The Problem

If the passion resides only in a few people at the top, what happens when they aren't there? What happens if they die or leave the organization? To be effective, passion—which is a very human quality—has to be built into the fabric of the organization, a very human institution.

Peter Senge and others have argued that the key to success is the learning organization. Still others, like Rosabeth Moss Kanter and Noel Tichy, have argued that the key is the teaching organization. Jerry Hirshberg has argued that it is the creative organization. All are correct in their belief that these are indeed critical items. But they are all by-products of the passionate organization. Without passion ingrained throughout the organization, the learning will turn into information gathering, the teaching into dry training, and the creativity into thin air.

Give us passion, and we will burn up the speedway. We will learn new stuff, blurt it out in our excitement, and find whole new things to learn about that we hadn't even thought of yesterday. We will teach so that we can learn and get feedback and generate new ideas for our beloved projects. And we will create new ways to learn and teach, new ways to think, new ways to find joy in the journey.

Encasing Passion

What do we mean by encasing passion?

To encase is to "enclose in or as if in a case." It means that we find something worthy in which to carry our passion. If there is no encasement, liberty can be abused, freedom can turn into license, and passion can run amok. As we said in Chapter 5, passion is uncontrollable; attempts to control it inevitably kill it or turn it sour. But it can be guided, and it *must* be guided.

The twin guides are vision and mutual trust.

Vision

We need to encase all our passions in our vision of the future, our understanding of our long-enduring purpose, our articulation and emphasis of die-for core values, and the practical development of goals that stir the soul.

This encasement needs to be our leader, bigger and more enduring than any individual person, no matter how intelligent or passionate, can ever be. Individual leaders are very important, since it is their
responsibility to embody this vision as well (we'll explore that idea in
Chapter 19). But the effective leader can only passionately *embody* the
vision; the leader can't *be* the vision. And it is everyone's responsibility to maintain and extend his or her passion about these encasements.

This is not a call for centralization of decentralized passionate
impulses. As we said earlier, the whole centralization versus decentralization argument is a phony one from the start. Of *course* we need
to have centralization, and of *course* we need to have decentralization.
The real question is, "Centralization by what?"

If we have centralization by structure, passion and enthusiasm
will die. We will be largely unable to hear the whispers of change
from the hinterlands and to act on them when we do. The organization will ossify and, given enough time, fossilize. Centralization by
structure always produces an either/or trade-off with necessary decentralization. Back and forth flows the power, tight and loose moves
the structure, but it is truly sound and fury, signifying nothing. It is a
colossal waste of human and other resources.

But if we have centralization by *vision*, passion and enthusiasm
will flourish, and we can be decentralized in our structure. Perma-
nently decentralized, with no more back and forth. We will be able
to pick up the nuances of the local customers and act on them
quickly and effectively. The organization can adjust and grow
organically, as needed. Vertical and horizontal integration can become seamless, because they are built around flexible ideas rather
than fixed power centers.

Centralization by vision requires no trade-off with decentralization. We can fully decentralize the structure without fear that doing
so will lead to chaos, because we have all committed to the relentless
pursuit of a future we all desire. We are pulled together by the unifying power of vision. The worst of our impulses (to limit and coerce)
can be replaced by the most noble (to free and inspire). We can have
our cake and eat it too.[1]

But for this to happen, our centralizing vision has to be a lot more
powerful and integrated than the typical "vision statement" that
hangs unread on the walls of far too many organizations. It has to be
a home-grown, agreed-upon, clear, compelling, ingrained picture of
the kind of organization we are and want to become.[2]

- *Home-grown.* The centralizing vision has to be grown from the bottom and nurtured from the top. The ideas and values are there. They may be incomplete, but everything that lives has to operate with some sense of what it is and what it wants to become. Even new organizational values come forth from, and have to align with, the best of what it means to be human. To grow the vision organically, with guidance and support from the organization's leaders, is the way to stirring victory.

- *Agreed-upon.* The vision can't be produced by consultants or top management and passed down the hierarchy. Even a big roll-out, with hoopla and fanfare, won't be enough to get full, passionate buy-in. The vision has to come from the bowels of the organization, from the best that lies within, from every corner and from every person who cares enough to let his or her voice be heard. Few organizations have been this thorough, this respectful of the humanity that makes up the organization. We can do it differently.

- *Clear.* The vision has to be conceived in such a way that it makes sense from both an external and an internal perspective. We can't afford to have anyone wonder what it means. This doesn't mean that it has to be short or sloganish—truly centralizing visions are neither simplistic nor stupid. But a clear vision should get an "of course" or "I see" response.

- *Compelling.* It has to be interesting, it has to be inspiring. It has to shake people up a bit, perhaps, but mainly it has to get them moving. There has to be something in it, something about it, that offers us a way to be better than we are.

- *Ingrained.* The vision has to be ingrained into the depths of the culture through massive, lavish communication, through consistent and thorough learning and teaching, and by allowing it to color and direct every decision, every day. We can have too much information—an overload—but we can't have too much communication, which is a primary attribute of human life and incredibly hard to realize in practice. Learning will work in the area of vision and values only when it is viewed as a process rather than an event and as an investment rather than a cost; values need to be part of all learning—even job skills learning—rather than taught as a separate "disconnected from the real work" course. And every decision has to be made in the light of what we want to become.

This centralization by vision is so critical that I want to elaborate on it in the next section. If we get this right, we'll have a lot less reorganizing, reengineering, and renovating in the years to come.

Vision and Strategy

Vision is a conception and statement of who we are and who we want to be—in other words, strategy and strategic thinking at the broadest and farthest-reaching level.

Vision is made up of two components:

1. *Our purpose.* Why do we exist? What do we hope to achieve? What would the world lose if we went out of business? Purpose is our *strategic vision.*
2. *Our values.* What are our core values? What makes us tick? What overrides all other considerations as we make or implement decisions? Values are our *cultural vision.*

Together, our purpose and values make up our vision of the future. In effect, this vision becomes our constitution. It informs, guides, and crystallizes our strategic thinking at the highest level, and our behaviors and mechanisms at the everyday level.

In the area of strategic thinking, the vision guides us as we ask the "four great questions":

1. What do we passionately care about that we do, or can do, better than anyone else? (internal strengths)
2. Does anyone out there care? (external opportunities)
3. What do we do poorly or in a way that is not aligned with our vision? (internal weaknesses)
4. Where are we vulnerable? (external threats)

This strategic thinking, which flows from our vision, has as its goal the generation of ideas, not numbers and forecasts. It helps us to innovate and to evaluate major changes in strategic direction. And it should be effective in preventing strategic planning from simply extrapolating the status quo.

Rational planning, informed by our strategic vision and related strategic thinking, can now set some intelligent objectives (for example, ROI, growth, profits, revenues, costs) and some stretch goals related to projects, programs, or products. The *deliberate strategy* that flows from rational planning allows the organizational leadership, using formal analysis processes, to plot in detail any new directions or continuations of legitimate current directions.

At the same time, however, our vision has also informed the culture through its statement of values and supporting behaviors, and by providing mechanisms to allow the organization as a whole to participate in the formulation of strategy. This *emergent strategy* comes from within the organization. It involves passion-led ideas, innovations, and creativity. This is the passionate side of strategy formation.

Both sides, the deliberate and the emergent, are necessary for success in our modern economy. Overemphasis on strategic planning has led organizations astray, taking them in some directions that were doomed to failure while missing golden opportunities living within the organization. To be sure, passionate ideas do arise even when they are not formally encouraged, but they are too often allowed to die from undernourishment, if they are not killed outright by the strategic planning process or inflexible organizational structures (and their related politics).

Taken together, deliberate strategy and emergent strategy can be merged into an *evolving organizational strategy*. This strategy formation process is more concerned with synthesis (pulling together ideas) than with analysis (dissecting ideas). It incorporates organizationwide involvement, supported by well-formed learning and communication processes. It is this evolving strategy that can then inform budgets and targets, programs, and daily actions. What we learn from these "working outs" of evolving strategy are fed back into the rational planning loop.

We have shown this process in diagram form in Table 12-1. As with all diagrams, not all relationships can be shown, but this illustrates that a truly effective vision, made up of a strategic vision stated as purpose and a cultural vision stated as core values, can and should guide *both the rational and the passionate sides of the organization*. It makes room for both deliberate and emergent strategy under the guidance of a centralizing vision.

By involving the insight and passion of all of our people, we can move from planning to true strategizing, and will continually reinvent our organization along the way—avoiding much of the need for massive reorganizing and reengineering efforts. "In almost all organizations," says strategy expert Dr. Gary Hamel, "planning is a highly elitist activity that takes place at the top of the company . . . [and involves] people who are deterministic, analytically trained, and distant from the voice of the customer. The process taps only a tiny percentage of an organization's total imagination."[3]

Table 12-1 Vision and Strategy

Vision is who we are and what we want to be—i.e., strategy and strategic thinking at the broadest and furthest-reaching level.

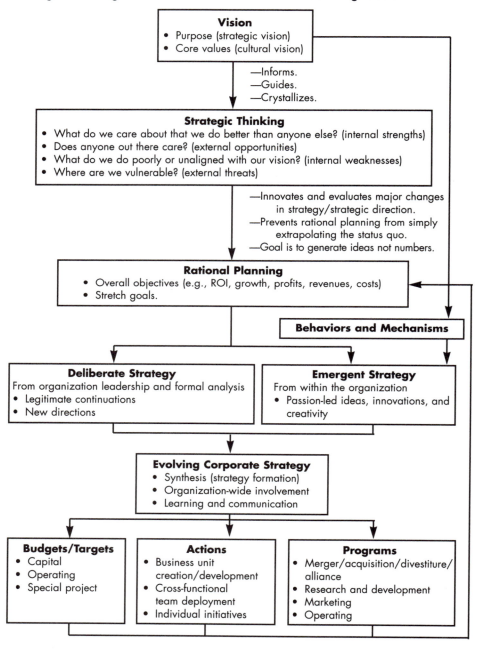

Behaviors and Mechanisms

A closer look at the cultural vision shows that the core values and their supporting behaviors and mechanisms are what encase the fire in daily life. "There's an old Jewish belief that you build a 'fence' around an impulse," says writer Norman Mailer.[4]

A core value that says, "We always listen to others' ideas fully before questioning them or presenting our own ideas" is a powerful statement of respect as well as an encasement of passion. No matter how excited I am about my idea, I can't present it until I first listen, and listen fully. I can't run roughshod over your ideas, picking them apart or trumping them with my own. That's just not who we are. We don't do things like that here.

Behaviors are clearly stated descriptions of what the core value *looks like* or *doesn't look like* in everyday practice. For example, on our core value of listening before talking, we could have the descriptions given in Table 12-2.

Table 12-2 also shows abbreviated lists of supporting behaviors for competence and for honesty and integrity. Most people don't want to work for an organization that tolerates or rewards incompetence while ignoring or devaluing competence. But what does this mean? Living the value by not blaming others would alone transform many organizations, eliminating the helplessness and scapegoating that can dramatically limit their effectiveness.

And to say that we prize honesty and integrity is to say a lot and not very much at the same time. This is a tremendous core value, perhaps the most important because it relates so deeply to who we really are and how we can work together in trust. But if we don't deal with what honesty means in the context of mistakes—we admit them, we learn from them, we don't bury them, we don't abuse those who make them—this core value will evaporate in the cauldron of daily human interaction.

Mechanisms are simple but consistently applied tools that ensure that the core value and supporting behaviors are practiced widely on a daily basis. On our core value of listening before talking, a very simple mechanism would be to have a reminder of the value at the top of the standard meeting agenda form. Another mechanism would be to have a "team health check" performed at the end of meetings or on some regular basis, and (among other things) ask if this value was practiced. We could also include questions about a person's living the value on a 360-degree feedback form.

Table 12-2   Supporting Behaviors for Core Values

Core Value	Supporting Behaviors	Nonsupporting Behaviors
Listening	• Team leaders always poll their team members on a topic, opportunity, or problem before expressing their own position. • Our first words are always "What do you think?" rather than "Here's what I think." • Questioning others is always done respectfully and with the intent to learn. • We present our own ideas with deference (not compromise) to what has already been said by others.	• We never use questions as an opportunity to put others on the spot or to teach our own position. • We never interrupt people rather than making a note of questions for an appropriate time. • We never present our ideas in a triumphal, "mine is the best" manner. • We do not disregard other people's concerns.
Competence	• We take ownership of our problems. • We ask for help when we need it. • We reward excellence. • We hire and/or promote for competence. • We take responsibility for our own development.	• We don't blame others. • We do a good job but are not arrogant about it. • We do not act as if we know everything. • We do not produce a product that we would not use ourselves.
Honesty and integrity	• We admit mistakes and use them as learning opportunities • We walk the talk. • We do what is right, not just what is legal. • When there are gray areas, we review them openly and make our concerns known. • We spend energy getting to the truth rather than covering it up.	• We never abuse anyone for an honest mistake. • We never falsify reports, records, etc. • We do not compromise on principles. • We do not promise what we cannot deliver. • We discourage behavior that is not aligned with our core values.

It takes time to design and build real-world mechanisms that are both simple to use and effective. It will take time to get feedback on them, hone them, discard some, and add others. But without the mechanisms, the values and behaviors will fade away or be reinterpreted to fit people's prejudices and preferences. Life and time and entropy will take their toll. On the other hand, if we take the time to build the culture that we really want and need, and if we provide both the forum in which passion can flourish and the tools to keep it pruned, we can become an ever more dominant force in the marketplace.

The Circle

A powerful vision does more than encase, guide, and direct passion. It *adds* to the passion. "If it's done well, the vision will inspire and provide the energy to achieve what the shared vision has defined," says Tom Isle, Vision Team leader at Potlatch Corporation. "Vision can lead us to achievements we never before thought possible," adds team facilitator Scott Dean.

By helping people see a better future, the vision can help them believe this future is attainable and worth being passionate about. This kind of big dream can inspire extraordinary effort. It can create a sense of urgency: "Look where we want to be, and look where we are right now." It can even affect our ability to hire and retain excellent people. In a recent survey of 25,000 employees, 64 percent said that a "clear sense of organizational purpose" would influence their choice of employer.[5]

Vision isn't hope, but it can give people something to hope for. The highest levels of passion come from the highest level of dedication to a compelling vision.

Mutual Trust

"The inability to create a shared vision and mutual trust are the main obstacles to building passion in an organization," Roy Coleman, Harley-Davidson director of manufacturing projects, told me. "I can't become passionate about something that I can't embrace. And I can't embrace something that I don't understand. And I can't embrace it with a group of people that I don't trust."

Tom Isle of Potlatch told me that the three main obstacles to building passion are "lack of trust, lack of trust, and lack of trust." Surveys we have done confirm that the "trust gap" is usually the biggest interpersonal barrier to an exciting future.

What are some of the key elements of building mutual trust?

Attitude of Respect

Trust has to begin with a fundamental respect for other people—even though some of them don't deserve it. We have to believe that people are responsible adults who really do want to achieve great goals and make a difference. A certain amount of trust has to be *granted*.

A Sure Walk of a Pure Talk

It's not just walking the talk. We have to walk in a sure manner, which means that we do it when it feels good and when it hurts, we keep our promises and commitments, and we apologize when we make mistakes. It means even more: We have to base all of our daily actions, even the little ones, on deeply held, unchangeable core values. The talk has to be pure, with no hedging. A certain amount of trust has to be *earned*.

Loathing of Hidden Agendas, Wide Sharing of Information

People will always know when we're holding something back. Even if we can't share it right now, if we suspect that they suspect, we at least need to let them know that there's *something*. And wide sharing of information—from one process to another, at meetings of natural work groups, with guests from other groups, at town meetings—is crucial. A certain amount of trust comes from being an *insider*.

Partnering

Trust is built through thrashing out problems and opportunities as partners. This means that hierarchy is put away with slide rules and eight-track tapes, and authority belongs to the group that is wrestling with the issue. Everyone is free to make honest assessments of other people and their ideas and plans, regardless of their formal positions in the organization. No relationship can fully prosper with an imbalance of power as its dominating premise. A certain amount of trust comes from being an *equal.*

Persisting

There will always be questions and doubts that can eat away at trust. When did they really learn about that merger? Did he honestly not know about that policy? What did she really say to that customer? Gossip and rumor mills can be formidable enemies to trust and can damage even good relationships. We have to be willing to give the benefit of the doubt, to ask clarifying questions, and to opt out of the gossip chain. A certain amount of trust needs to be *fought for.*

The Future of Organizational Design

All organizations are designed, either deliberately or by circumstance, to perform at their current level.

The rational approach to organizational design is to build around systems and structures. Any other approach wouldn't be rational. We lay out, select, and choose processes that will, we think, achieve our objectives (product quality, cycle time, customer satisfaction, etc.). Then we put structures in place (business units, divisions, departments, product lines, project teams, matrices) to support those systems. As time goes on, we further rationalize the design with policies, procedures, job descriptions, and performance evaluations. The result is weighty and perhaps cumbersome, but it can get the job done. Sometimes, the job gets done in spite of the design.

There are many problems with this approach to organizational design.

- With an organization of any size, we just aren't smart enough to think about and think through all the systems and all their nuances.
- The systems only approximate reality in the first place, and as reality changes, our elaborately designed systems can get farther and farther from the marketplace, and eventually have no connection to reality at all. The system becomes the end rather than the means. Budgeting processes, for example, can consume vast amounts of energy to produce an outcome that is largely rubber-stampism.

- The structures can become so ponderous and oppressive that they become an actual barrier to making necessary adjustments in the systems and processes. There is something inherently flawed in having multitudinous sign-offs to *simplify* a process.

- The structures can become the dominant part of the design and can dictate where the systems and processes should go, leading to "function follows form" rather than "form follows function."

- This can lead to the need for "reengineering," which could and should have been done as a normal, continual part of the organization's life rather than in a giant, intrusive program whose potential risks can outweigh its potential benefits.

- All of the above absorb massive resources and take way too long to happen to help us in our actual purpose, which is not to design and redesign organizations, but to meet stakeholder needs and add value to everything we touch.

The passionate approach to organizational design implies a very different set of criteria.

- The organization itself will pursue only what it is, or can be, passionate about.

- The vision of the organization, including its understanding of its purpose (its strategic vision) and its core values (its cultural vision), will revolve around these passions.

- We will spend less time asking about core competencies and more time asking about core passions. Just as individuals can be skilled at something about which they are not passionate, so organizations can fall into the same trap. We make it, but we hate it—or just don't care.

- Strategic thinking will shift from asking, "What do we do better than anyone else?" to asking, "What do we *care about* more than anyone else?" What *are* we passionate about? What are our people passionate about? Only after we ask these questions, and get good answers, should we attempt to match the answers with our core competencies and the needs of the marketplace. If we care, we either have or can acquire the skills. If we care, some people in the marketplace will probably care, too. We begin to let what we believe in drive what we do, rather than letting what we do drive what we believe.

- We will hire people who are passionate about the *same* vision and values and about *different* issues and directions.

- We will allow the systems and processes and structures to be more fluid, to be changed or discarded *as we go* by people who really care about results more than about methods.

- We will replace systems with agreed-upon vision and mutual trust, and organization charts with natural work groups and partnering. We won't bother to write or replace policy and procedures manuals or job descriptions.

The need to design organizations using a passionate rather than a rational approach becomes *more* critical as the organization grows. If the growth is an extension of our current organization, continuous adjustments along the way, as needed, can be made by the passionate organization, but much less so by a structured organization.

If the growth is through a merger or acquisition, a whole new level of challenge arises. All too often, the focus in these actions is on the rational side: How do we blend these two organizations? Where do we have duplication and overlap, and how do we eliminate it? Who should take what positions? Who reports to whom? How do we combine our marketing efforts? How should we streamline operations? These aren't bad questions; they're just not the place to start, and they're not enough.

Mergers and acquisitions seldom, if ever, founder on these issues. They *do* struggle because the real passions of the organizations and people within them are not taken into account, fully evaluated, or made a priority during the transition. The transaction ends up becoming passion's black hole.

Even someone as sensitive to people and relationships as Stephen Covey can miss this, as has been evidenced by the massive internal problems experienced in a merger between his organization (Covey Leadership Center) and Franklin Quest. "Covey claimed the inherent organizational *expertise* (emphasis added) would create a model merger"—a typical rational expectation. "Greg Link, head of business development [says], 'The stark reality is that mergers are tough. It takes people time to adapt.'. . . Executing a new core mission has proved troublesome, too. Rather than complementing each other, [they] clashed and caused infighting."[6] In a survey of 218 major U.S. organizations, "integrating organizational cultures was the top challenge for 69 percent of the surveyed companies."[7]

The process is more like two people with children marrying than it is a calculated plan. The process needs time: to discern and work on the negative passions that are guaranteed to be there, to find and build on the points where passions align, to discover ways to blend apparent but not deep misalignments, to neutralize or eliminate the areas about which the whole new organization cannot be passionate, to build a new vision from scratch, and to weave a whole new fabric of mutual trust. Franklin Covey originally planned, and then abandoned, a slower integration process that could have prevented many of its post-merger problems.

In a merger or acquisition, we need a new visioning process and a team to steer it. We need to do in-depth culture surveys and take the results seriously. We need to have massive and open *two-way* communication that includes every member of the new "family." We need to lose our illusions about "natural synergies" and people being "reasonable." And we need to focus first on the passions and second on the plans.

Conclusion

As we design our organizations, we have to get the structure out of the way. But we can't simply let everything run loose. We have to centralize by vision, by our purpose and core values, and by the strategic, value-adding goals that derive from them. We have to guide, direct, and align our people with our vision, purpose, values, and goals by the use of well-thought-out and consistently practiced enablers (behaviors and mechanisms). And all of this has to take place in a trust-rich environment if it is to flourish.

The traditional management functions were planning, organizing, directing, and controlling. People need to do these things, but for themselves, not for others (regardless of how small the span of control). At the highest level, these functions are carried out best by a well-implemented vision and strategy. They will bring the deliberate plan and the emerging plan together in an evolving corporate strategy, organize our resources to achieve the plan, direct us toward where and who we want to be, and control our distractions and keep us from running amok.

Even more. A well-prepared vision embodies leadership. It is like a platform to a politician, though much more so because it contains enablers to make the platform reality. The vision guides the leader, and the leader, if aligned with the vision, is its living expression. Here's what we believe in. And see, here it is in practice.

ITT had no vision, only autocratic Hal Geneen. When Geneen was gone, so was the ITT that he built. Even decent leaders, in the final analysis, have left only a small mark if their work did not include production of a compelling vision. Chrysler without Lee Iacocca is a very different place *because* he is gone. In many ways, Iacocca (not any sort of compelling vision) *was* Chrysler.

Only the vision can live on. Even when great leaders, leaders who embody and live out the vision, die, the vision lives on—if they have shared it with their followers. Avis is still driven by the vision established decades ago under the leadership—and nurturing and inclusionary approach—of Bob Townsend. The vision survived his departure and lives on even though he is no longer with us. General Electric is likely to experience the same survivability of vision without Jack Welch, as are Southwest Airlines without Herb Kelleher and Marriott when its current family leadership is gone.

Vision, along with the underutilized powerhouse of mutual trust, is a force to be reckoned with.

And a suitable encasement for fire.

Notes

1. The first decision for any organization, of course, is, "Should we be doing this at all?" If it isn't related to the core of the business, including the core strategic vision and core competencies, it should be sold off or dismantled. If it is related to the core strategic vision but isn't a core passion or competence, it should be outsourced. What we are talking about in this section are functions that are related to the strategic vision and are, or can become, a core passion or competence. The use of "internal free markets," in which, say, the purchasing departments from each of our ten divisions compete with each other internally (and perhaps even provide services externally), can be a way to maximize this "centralization by vision, decentralization of structure" approach, but it can work effectively even without those "free markets" if we have a compelling enough vision.
2. For more information on how to test the reality and value of your vision after it's developed, see Chapter 4 of my book *Fatal Illusions: Shredding a Dozen Unrealities That Can Keep Your Organization From Success* (New York: AMACOM, 1997).
3. As reported in *Leadership*, November 1998, p. 2.
4. As quoted in *Booknotes* (New York: Times Books, 1997), p. 162.
5. Study by William M. Mercer Inc., as reported in *HRFocus*, September 1998, p. 5.
6. "Gurus: Do As I Say, Not As I Do," *USA Today*, December 7, 1998.
7. As reported in *Management Review*, January 1999, p. 6.

13

Building Passion
for Stakeholders

Treat the customer as an appreciating asset.

—Tom Peters, *Thriving on Chaos*

People come here [her store] to brighten up. . . . We want people to feel the electricity.

—Nancy Schrag, owner, Seasons, *Gift Reporter*

To satisfy the customer is the mission and purpose of every business.

—Peter Drucker

One of the most difficult missions for leaders to accomplish is to get their people to care about somebody else.

The norm in life is for people to look out for their own interests. This is good as far as it goes. Personal responsibility and initiative are excellent traits, all too lacking in far too many organizations, cultures, and nations. Within some constraints—the rule of law, human and civil rights, a sense of justice and equity—Adam Smith's "invisible hand" really does work. Although imperfect, it works more efficiently and effectively than any other economic system discovered or conjured up by human beings.

Economic systems guided by something other than the invisible hand have not been nearly as successful. Nations are always being tempted by the supposed advantages of planning. If "chaos" (freedom) works pretty well, just think what planning can do. But planning has proved to be the most colossal failure when attempted at the most colossal levels. The totally planned economies—communist, socialist, or otherwise—not only have not produced any wealth but have destroyed whatever value existed when they arrived. The commandeer and control economies—fascist, oligarchical, or otherwise—have produced some wealth for consumption by the military during a war or by the top dogs during peaceful times, but nothing for everyone else. Even in the "collaborative" economies, such as Japan, where government, business, labor, and financial powers supposedly work together to produce something better than is possible in unplanned economies, the results have been immobility and stagnation.

So an economy or organization that provides for, allows for, *insists on* its people's taking responsibility for their own decisions, actions, directions, successes, and failures is the best possible option for the people who work in it.

The problem arises when people's own issues remain their sole, or even primary, focus.

The *way* individuals achieve their personal goals is *always* by meeting the needs of somebody else. No job, group, team, or organization exists in a void, merely to satisfy its own needs and desires. *The way to personal success is to make others successful.* If we solve somebody's problems better than anyone else, if we *care* more about somebody's problems more than anyone else, we are value adders for that person and wealth builders for ourselves.

Ultimately, great leaders need to nurture a passion for stakeholders. We don't just want our people to be excited; we want them to be excited about someone else, and about what they can do for that someone else that perhaps no one else can do as well. A passion for success or a passion for excellence falls short of the greatest passion, which is a passion for others. This great passion leads directly to both personal success and excellence.

We can't *get* people to be passionate about stakeholders, but we can create an environment in which passionate people are free and willing to jump in headlong.

A Passion for Customers

Who are these people that provide us with our organizational lifeblood?

Customers come in many forms, all of which can lead us to

passion, as we become aware of their needs and devoted to meeting these needs and exceeding their expectations.

Some of our customers are with us by choice. They have searched the market thoroughly and have determined that ours is the organization that is most likely to satisfy their needs. They feel like such a perfect fit, the relationship seems so easy and natural, that we can easily take them for granted. We need to remember that they still have a choice. We should start every year by asking ourselves the key question, "If they weren't already our customers, what would it take to win them?"—and then we should do it.

Some people have been our customers for a long time, and they keep coming back because of inertia. They're customers by habit. They will keep coming back even if we're mediocre, as long as we don't mess up too badly or a really excellent organization doesn't aggressively seek their business. We need to dread comments like, "Oh, they're good for 50,000 again this year." No customer's business is that certain. We should find out which of their other wants and needs we're not currently satisfying or even aware of. Once again, we have to approach them passionately, as though they weren't current customers.

Some customers are with us by accident. They may not even know why they're buying from us. Maybe we were just there or convenient when they first realized they had a need. These customers are really easy to lose. We've got to develop an internal rationale for why they should buy from us and no one else, and then press forward enthusiastically with that program.

Airlines, trucking companies, telephone companies, and others have all had their day of having captive customers, because people needed what they were offering and found themselves dealing with a government-created monopoly. It would be contrary to human nature for monopolistic organizations to seek to perform for their customers at the highest possible level. Passion is virtually absent, because it has no reason to exist. In fact, few organizational forms are as deadly in killing off passion as a monopoly. The strongest passion they create is a passion on the part of their customers to demand deregulation (read: getting rid of your damnable monopoly). If I were managing a monopoly, I would do everything I could to eliminate this unfair and deadening condition, because nothing is more stultifying than "we don't have to, so we won't." It's a long, slow death.

For most of us, only a very small percentage of our possible customers are buying from us. How can we be passionate about noncustomers when we don't even know who they are? But this is the key: We have to find out who they are and get excited about them today, maybe long before they choose to buy from us. In the 1970s, when I was with one of the largest engineering consulting firms in the world, I watched one partner spend more than five years grooming a potential client—preparing proposal after proposal, doing small and unprofitable "dog work," and generally just staying close. His passion finally paid off with a huge, multiyear contract from one of the largest electric utilities in the midwestern part of the United States. Ultimately, his passion was irresistible.

How do we get our people to be passionate about all of these different types of customers? There are some things we can do.

- *Tell stories.* We need to tell our people a lot of stories about our customers, particularly focusing on how our customers are using our products and services to meet their needs. We have to tie our people into the sequence of servanthood: We serve others, who serve others, who serve others. We've got to find a way to make these customers very real and worthwhile to all our people, regardless of their job or function. Our customers need to be seen in their humanity.

- *Distribute customer literature.* We can take the best of our customers' literature—sales brochures, annual reports, internal newsletters—and disperse it widely inside our organization. Who are these people? What are they trying to do? The more real they are to me, the more I can care about them. And if our people have a lot of information about customers, they can work much more responsibly and creatively, as well as enthusiastically.

- *Expose everyone to customers.* Too many organizations have taken the approach that only management or sales should have contact with customers. How can our people care about customers when those customers are a black box? We should expose our people—all our people—to customers in different settings—our place and theirs, over the phone and over the Internet—as much as possible. Someone who we fear will be a disaster with a customer is someone who needs to be trained, fixed, or terminated. "When your people get to know their customers firsthand, they will try to please them, because if you know someone and he is your friend, you will try to make him happy," says Tom Isle of Potlatch Corporation. Customers need to have a face.

- *Survey customers and distribute results to everyone.* We have to ask our customers often what they *feel* and not just what they think. We have to sniff out the underlying negative feelings that could cause them to go elsewhere. And all of us doing this is better than a few of us doing it.

- *Role play.* We can put our people in the position of being our customer. Role playing, where our people act the part of a customer, can go far toward showing people how best to meet customer needs. Creative simulations, where others try to sell these "customers," can sharpen everyone's perspective. And you have to love it to see it. Ultimately, everyone who works for us has to love our product or service if they are going to make it the very best it can possibly be.

- *Consider everyone to be performance consultants.* We can create forums where diverse perspectives can be brought to bear on the performance level of our products or services in meeting our customers' needs. What problems are they having? How could we improve performance even where there is no obvious problem? We need a passion for solving problems, both current and potential.

- *Make everyone futurists.* We can create forums for "blue-sky" thinking. We can expect everyone to be futurists and researchers and trend-watchers. Where is our customers' industry going? What will they need from us when it gets there? To be on the cutting edge, we need all of our people to have a passion for our customers' future.

- *Define clearly who the customer is.* Not knowing who the customer is can be a big problem. Is it the one who buys my product or the one who uses it? Is it the initial user or the ultimate user? This can be especially challenging for not-for-profit organizations. Is our customer the one giving us the money? The one whose needs we are attempting to meet? The community? We can't have passion for our customers if we don't know who they are.

- *Treat employees like customers.* We can practice on each other. "It's very rare to see a manager who treats his customers one way and his employees another. And it's awfully hard for employees to treat customers well if the boss treats them badly."[1] Treatment of others is a way of living that is hard to compartmentalize.

- *Fire the stinkers.* Some customers are perfectly designed to kill our organization's passion. We've got to get rid of them before they do it. Warren Buffet says that he "won't do business with anyone who makes my stomach churn."

For far too many people, the customer is a faceless, impersonal blob. No one can be passionate about a blob. We should give our customers form, and watch the care and passion grow. *Everyone* should be able to answer the question, "What do our customers really want?"

A Passion for Shareholders

Some people have chosen to invest their precious, scarce resources in our organization and its ideas. How can we not be passionate about them?

And yet this is very often the case. Sometimes we fear investors: What will they do? Will they stay with us? Will they bail out at the first sign of bad or even average news? But mostly we take them for granted. We've got their money. We'll try to give them a decent return. That should be enough.

But it isn't enough. We need to encourage passion for those who have voted for us with their money. We should want them to believe that investing anywhere else is long-term bad judgment. And, as with noncustomers, we should get to know our noninvestors, and ask what it will take to cause them to beat a path to our door.

How can we encourage passion for shareholders (all of this works very nicely for not-for-profit organizations if we substitute the word "contributor" or "supporter")?

• *Profile investors.* Who are these people? How can we care if they have no face? These profiles can be generic ("15 percent of our investors are widows and orphans") or they can be specific ("Here is Rachel Valins, who gave us these three reasons why she has entrusted her savings to us").

• *Meet investors.* Let different people attend shareholders' and board of directors' meetings. We're all just *people,* for heaven's sake. I want my production and sales and accounting people to be thinking about some very real, living, breathing human beings when they are making key decisions about spending those people's money.

- *Differentiate investors.* Our people need to see the difference in attitudes, expectations, and commitment between individual investors (investing their own money) and institutional investors (investing other people's money). Each of these groups needs further differentiation. The goals are understanding, awareness of needs, and a higher level of passion in meeting those needs.

- *Think of investors as customers.* In a very real way, investors are customers, albeit a very special category. We can use the current "customer thinking" of our people to our advantage in meeting the needs of our investors. What is our market share? How do we improve it? How do our investors define quality? What would they consider to be a good value?

- *Make employees researchers.* We can encourage all our employees to ask their family, friends, and others some important questions: "What would it take to get you to invest in my organization? What would prevent you from making this decision?" Where and why people spend their money gets down to some very core issues. Collect this information systematically, and it will provide you with an excellent database for decision making—and a lot of people who are thinking about what it takes to succeed in the financial marketplace.

- *Treat employees like CEOs.* We have to create an environment in which everyone sees himself as a mini-CEO. Employees need to see themselves as trustees and stewards of other people's resources. If we want them to act as if it's their business, we have to make it their business. Everyone should lead something—a project team, a problem-solving effort, an investment evaluation effort, or a resource allocation decision—at least once a year.

- *Connect employees at the pocketbook.* As much as possible, we should tie individual and collective financial incentives for our employees to our return to our shareholders. It is hard for people not to care deeply about shareholder value when their own financial future is connected to it.

- *Turn employees into shareholders.* When we convert employees into shareholders, we improve their understanding of the shareholders' perspective and create a very personal incentive to make it better.

Shareholders are the great invisible entity in organizational life. We can't live without them, but just who the heck are they, anyway?

If our people can answer that question satisfactorily, we've got most of the competition beat.

A Passion for Helpers

Helpers come in many forms: vendors, suppliers, contractors, lawyers, accountants, consultants. They make their living by helping us make our living.

Why should we have a passion for them? We're paying them, aren't we? Isn't that enough?

It's enough if we want to have a business relationship. But it misses the mark by a mile if we want to have a passionate relationship, one that helps us extend ourselves to new heights.

The worst attitude we can have is one of superiority: "They need us more than we need them." This can lead us to try to extract everything we can from them, use them, make unreasonable demands. Replacing them is no big deal, because it's "just business."

No, it's just dumb.

These people are *helpers.* They can help us be a whole lot better than we already are, or than we can be without them. But we have to value their help, appreciate their help, celebrate and recognize them for their help. My feeling is that all my helpers can help me more than they already are. They know things they haven't told me, they have products or services or technical expertise that isn't out on the table. They have tacit knowledge and street smarts. How do I get these things working for me? How do I get my helpers' *passion* working for me?

I have to be passionate about my helpers. I have to abandon the concept of a business relationship. I have to get my people to believe that there is something in this relationship that is so valuable that they would be crazy to miss it.

How do we do this?

• *Choose terrific helpers.* There's no way that people can be passionate about nincompoops. Get rid of the losers and the mediocre and the arrogant and the pains in the neck. Have helpers worthy of your organization's passion.

• *Get everyone involved.* We can avoid the logical but restrictive practice of letting only certain people select and work with helpers. We can expose everyone to the selection process, and the deselection process. Cross-training by working with helpers is a mind-opening process.

• *Make everyone a helper.* We can put everyone in the position of being an internal helper—a supplier to another department, a consultant to a project team. In this capacity, each employee can make proposals and presentations. Helping is a state of mind, not a position. No external helper can long exist with an attitude of "you owe me"—and yet many organizations try to exist when they are chock full of people who have no helper orientation, who really do believe that the organization "owes" them. Many organizations talk about internal customers, but if we haven't established a culture that requires people to really act like helpers—if helping isn't a core value—it's all just so much talk.

To sum up, we want to be passionate about our helpers because that will cause them to help us more, and because it will create an orientation toward helping inside our organization.

A Passion for the Food Chain

What we do will always affect more than customers, shareholders, and helpers. It will have an impact on communities, the economy, the culture, and future generations.

If we can generate passion for these unseen groups, we will extend our own vision and create passion for our organization "out there."

How can we take this giant step?

• *Make them visible.* We have to talk about these groups when we discuss future plans and decisions. And the more specific we can be, the more real they will become and the greater the passion we will feel for them. "We anticipate adding 2,000 jobs to the local economy, which should finally allow the community to complete plans for the new high school and community hospital." Specific stories of individuals who will be helped add mightily to the effect.

• *Sell the organization's merits.* We can equip all of our people to be spokespeople for the organization to these groups. Public relations departments should be *teaching* operations, not *doing* operations. Nothing builds passion and understanding faster or more effectively than having to carry the message to outsiders who come with doubts and questions, if not hostility.

• *Determine their needs and wants.* We may do market surveys, supplier surveys, and maybe even shareholder surveys, but do we do community surveys? We have to find out what these people desire. We may not be able to meet it, but knowing what it is and including it in our strategy can extend our perspective and build our passion.

• *Consider the impact.* In talking about the impact of our decisions on all these groups, we increase our ability to care about them. No organization lives in a vacuum. A passion for our total context can make us more valuable than perhaps we can even imagine.

Evaluate Passion for Stakeholders

How do our people stand in terms of passion for stakeholders?

Is she excited about customer X? Where's our proof? (Passion always leaves a trail.) If there's no passion, what's the problem? Is it personal entropy? If so, we need to find the cause and correct it immediately. No customer will long abide being treated as a burden or a nuisance. Or is customer X a passion killer? If a lot of our people don't love customer X, something needs to go—a lot of people or one customer. "Love them or leave them" should be our motto. Some customers should be treasured, some accepted, some put on probation—and a few put out of our misery.

What we're saying is this: If passion is missing from stakeholder relationships, we have a really serious problem. Duty will be insufficient as a driver in the kind of economic war all of us are and will be engaging in. Something has to change. Something is out of whack. Either our values are off, our matching isn't working, or our stakeholders don't understand our values or our vision.

When we evaluate our stakeholder relationships through the grid of passion, we expose all sorts of questions and issues and problems that the rational model can't even see. "What do you think?"—the question of the twentieth-century organization—must give way to the inquiry of the twenty-first: "What do you feel?"

If nothing, that's bad. If negative, that's deadly.

As leaders, we must evaluate the level of passion for stakeholders, and act passionately on the results.

Conclusion

Passion is not just an internal force.

At its highest level, passion reaches out, absorbing others in its fire and generating fires about us in others' hearts. To build this passion, we have to know these stakeholders, these outsiders, and care about their needs and desires and problems. They have to become real to us, in as specific a form and fashion as possible.

A passionate organization is a dominant competing force.

One that is passionate about all its stakeholders joins the ranks of the unstoppable.

Note

1. Carl Sewell and Paul B. Brown, *Customers for Life: How to Turn That One-Time Buyer Into a Lifetime Customer* (New York: Pocket Books, 1990), p. 119.

14

Stoke the Fire of Waning Passion

Honest criticism means nothing: what one wants is unrestrained passion, fire for fire.

—Henry Miller, *Sexus*

If you aren't fired with enthusiasm, you will be fired with enthusiasm.

—Vince Lombardi, former head coach, Green Bay Packers

Success depends on getting the maximum possible energy out of everyone in the organization and channeling that energy to achieve positive results.

—Noel M. Tichy, *The Leadership Engine*

Why are dispassionate people that way? Is it because there is something wrong with them, or because there is something wrong with the organization? How can we tell which is which? What do we do about it?

Some people are dispassionate—without passion—because there *is* something wrong with them. Some have been taught, by word and deed, that expressing emotion is inappropriate or even wrong. Some have been taught that even having the emotions is wrong. Others have had bitter experiences, and have assumed the role of victim rather than rallying and making a comeback. Perhaps they have simply never found what it is that would stir their souls. Regardless of what happened before, however, being passionless is a choice. We can choose to be dead, or we can choose to be alive.

Avoid the Myth of Motivation

The first thing to do when we sense that passion is waning in someone is to avoid buying into the myth of motivation. This myth says that we can motivate people to do what they aren't doing and aren't even giving a sign of wanting to do. It says that motivation is primarily our problem, not theirs. And it misses the reality that the only motivation worth talking about is *self*-motivation, as shown in Table 14-1. "The first secret of motivation is that nobody else can motivate you," says Dave Yoho.[1]

Table 14-1   The Myth Versus the Truth of Motivation

The Myth: Other-Driven	*The Truth:* Self-Driven
External: Motivation depends on our pushing people to perform.	*Internal:* Motivation depends on people's pushing themselves to perform.
Scheme: It is our job as leaders to tinker until we find a motivational system that works.	*Environment:* It is our job as leaders to create a climate in which passion can live and not die.
Grand plan: We search the literature to find the perfect, one-size-fits-all approach to motivation.	*Mass customization:* We nurture a multifaceted approach that reaches each person at his or her self-motivated center.
Lock picking: If we persist, we can "crack," "recode," and discover the way to make them run.	*Door knocking:* If we are paying attention, we can knock on people's hearts in such a way that they will choose to open the door.

There are more books on motivating employees than can be read, or perhaps even counted. I've generally stopped reading them. If I have people who just don't care, who aren't intrinsically excited about what they're doing, no amount of rewards and recognition will bring about deep and lasting passion. They may respond for a bit because they enjoy being rewarded and recognized, but the glow will fade fast if they have no inherent passion.

Rewards and recognition are important, but as a capstone rather than as a cornerstone. They are a fitting conclusion to the end of a successful race, but not the reason to run. Olympic champions do focus on winning a medal, but that isn't the reason why they run. They run because they love it, because they have to, because they can't live without it. In fact, only this level of passion can carry an athlete through the years of grueling preparation that are necessary in order to win the prize. No one at that level is running simply because she is good at running.

One respondent to a survey we were tabulating for a manufacturing organization said, "There's nothing you can do to help me reach my goals or be passionate about this job. This kind of work is inherently boring, and there's not much you or anyone else can do about it." But the respondent was wrong. There *is* something that can be done—two things, in fact: First, bored individuals can be helped to find work that stirs their souls, either here or elsewhere; and second, someone (it's guaranteed) can be found out there who will find or make this so-called boring job thoroughly exciting. The problem is usually the *match,* not the *work.*

Other respondents said, "We want to advance in our careers, but there just isn't opportunity for us." But there is *always* opportunity to do or be something if we love it enough. There are no silver platters— but there are lots of silver opportunities.

Once someone has chosen to be dead, we are very, very limited as to what we can do in the workplace to help them revive. We can't revive them. Even helping them is a monumental task. Few adults who have lived for a long time without passion will probably ever revive. The ones who do come back to life will do so as a result of a personal journey, a willingness to face reality, a refusal to stay dead.

We should thank our people, reward our people, recognize our people. It's the right thing to do, the decent thing to do, the fitting thing to do. They will appreciate it. But doing those things won't create passion—ever. They are the gravy on the potatoes.

Passion is the potatoes.

Stoking the Fire

Having recognized that motivation isn't our responsibility, we can still take a number of steps to stir (never instill) the passion in people whose enthusiasm is waning, as long as they still have a spark glowing somewhere inside them.

Rest

Human beings are biological systems, among other things. As we discussed in Chapter 10, nothing living functions well without rest and regeneration. The most productive and creative thing we can do is to insist that our people truly rest from their work on a regular and cyclical basis. This means that we give them at least one day a week completely free of work and organizational demands. Theoretically, most workers are on a five-day workweek, which would yield two days of rest; in practice, many people never really have a break. They take work home, make and receive phone calls, get called into meetings, and attend social events as networking opportunities. Sometimes we do it to them; sometimes they do it to themselves. But the human engine is not a perpetual-motion machine. It will burn out.

The same is true for the bigger cycles of life. Most organizations take stock of where they are on a quarterly basis. What have we been doing? What do we need to change? Where do we want to take this thing? Individuals are no different. People need to take stock and ask the same questions, and it's very hard to do so on the job or in a typical packed weekend. I like to encourage people to split up part of their vacation time into four quarterly regroupings—extended weekends, preferably away from home with all of its projects and demands. People also need a real vacation once a year, during which they can think about their work but not about their jobs.

And we shouldn't overlook rest during the day, either. Too few people are comfortable taking a walk, reading a magazine, or staring out the window. A day has energy cycles; rest when we are at a low ebb is an investment, not a distraction. Michael Jordan is one of the best athletes of the last hundred years, but without rest during the game he has been much less useful (and sometimes even counterproductive) at the end of the game.

"Recreation is a second creation, when weariness has almost annihilated one's spirits," wrote French cleric Thomas Fuller. "It is the breathing of the soul, which otherwise would be stifled with continual business." A person whose passion is waning may need a gently forced sabbatical, taken without penalty, to do a tune-up.

Recharging

Time and life can take their toll. There are mistakes and failures, horrible customers, rotten people. If this is the cause of the flagging passion, we can do something to reinvigorate the person. We need to shake such people up, move them around, move them away. "Constant labor of one uniform kind destroys the intensity and flow of a man's . . . spirits, which find recreation and delight in mere change of activity," wrote Karl Marx. The grass isn't greener in the new position, but at least it's different. We can't afford to run a thoroughbred into the ground.

Volunteering

We can offer the person a number of assignments, a portfolio of possible jobs. Watch her read the list, or listen to your description, and see when her eyes light up. She will make a difference on the projects that put fire in her eyes.

We have to let people know that there is no longer any "it all pays the same" kind of thinking. They can't just show up and expect good pay, benefits, and conditions. There is no point in being a victim and complaining about life, leadership, or anything else.

Unions have far too often fallen prey to this scapegoating of others to excuse their lack of passion. Far too often, their passion has been for defending seniority systems and old ways that do anything but advance unions as a viable global force. One twenty-year union veteran, a hard-working floor leader, told me, "If we didn't have the union, a lot of my friends would be fired." When I asked him if they needed to be fired, his answer (after a pause) was, "Yes." In talking with a high-ranking officer of a major international union, I asked how the members felt about partnering with management. His response was insightful: "A lot of people just want things to stay the same. They really don't see that the world has changed. But we've got to do things differently. If we don't find a way to partner with the companies our people work at, those companies aren't going to be competitive and there won't be any jobs to worry over the seniority of. We've got to get excited about being the best union working for the best companies."

Instead of worrying about jobs being exported, unions need to work on how to transform as many of their status quo blue-collar workers as possible into passionate knowledge workers. Leaders need to persuade their members that they can't fight against the flow of history and the marketplace. It's either learn and change and get excited or perish. They can fight against reality, or they can get on the cutting edge of reality. Some unions and their leaders are going to get on the cutting edge. They are going to be a value-added component of their organizations, and they won't have to fight for the jobs of an ever-shrinking pool of "senior" workers, or fight to keep work around that is an economic absurdity.

Intrapreneuring

Not boundaryless. Not centerless.
Polycentric.
To operate without boundaries, personally or organizationally, leads to confusing enmeshment rather than vital connection. It can leave us unable to set goals, make decisions, or simply say no. To operate without a center, personally or organizationally, leads to loss of direction rather than vibrant flow. It can leave us unable to see the goals, take responsibility and accountability, and feel successful in what we are doing.

To be polycentric simply means to be many-centered. Each person is a basic center, complete with boundaries that connect with others. Each person who walks through that door has to feel as if he or she is CEO of his or her own business. How can I not be passionate if I am running my own show?

To be polycentric means having natural work groups form around their own centers. These groups could be self-directed work teams, project teams, or business units. We stop trying to impose structure, either the older structure of functional divisions or the newer structure of the learning organization.

To be polycentric means to build a federation that encourages local passion. Inside our organizations, we need neither the strong national governments of the twentieth century nor the isolated city-states of medieval Italy or ancient Greece. This is already occurring in the political/economic sphere, as polycentric regions push past the older structures of city and state. According to cultural observer Robert Kaplan,

> Orange County is America's most fully evolved urban pod. . . . Already the western Kansas City suburbs [where I live and work] . . . are called Johnson County, and the prosperous Maryland suburbs of Washington, D.C. are called Montgomery County. . . . [Orange] County comprises twenty-eight separate municipalities, many with their own centers. The term "suburb" does not properly describe this advanced, polycentric urban pod. Because these centers do not resemble traditional downtowns, they are overlooked by people whose eyes have yet to adjust to the post-industrial age.[2]

Some organizations are moving in the same direction, creating smaller offices throughout a city or region rather than big, visually impressive campuses. Components of organizations (like sales) can take the same approach. The goal is to take people out of "jobs" and "positions" and put them in the center of a real, thriving, mini-organization.

As leaders in organizations, we need to adjust our eyes. We must have boundaries. We must have centers. But where will they be? And how will they best interact?

As much as possible, we need to stoke the fire by letting everyone, individually and in their natural work groups, feel the same pressures as any organizational CEO.

Obstacles to Passion

As much as we hate to admit it, sometimes the reason why passion is waning in our people can be found in our own mirrors. There are many things organizations do that restrict and kill passion. Here are some of the worst, and what we can do about them.

Mismatch

We have built our organization on the rational plan, and we have people who are horribly mismatched with their great enthusiasms. There is no outlet for their passion, so it atrophies from disuse. As we've stressed before, good matching is critical, for them and our organization.

Drown Out Enthusiastic Voices

Most organizations are like massive filters, designed to squeeze the truth (especially the painful part) out of ideas as they go up the line. I'm passionate, but you don't even know I exist—so why should I care? Worse, any good ideas that do make it to the top are not credited to the person who came up with them. It's hard to be passionate when you're stealing from me. We have to build mechanisms so that all voices are heard—360-degree reviews, surveys, face-to-face meetings with those in formal authority. People quit voting, and caring, when they don't think their input makes any difference.

Crush Dissent

Some cultures are designed, like a fragile, clinging, monarchy, to crush dissent. We give dissenters no hearing. Complaints are not welcome, or even heard. Passionate disagreement is written off as a bad attitude or assaulted as a personality conflict. We say we value diversity, but we don't mean it. What we mean is that we value the diversity required by *law* (race, gender, age), but we loathe diversity of *opinion* and *perspective*—which no law can force us to value. We tear into anything that is fiery, radical, or different. We tap into the destructive power of sarcasm and ridicule. The result? All silent on the western front. This obstacle could be alleviated if people had some opportunity, such as an organizational ombudsman or a method of due process, to safely breach the chain of command.

Discourage Spontaneity

Rational organizations fear the dreaded spontaneous comment or criticism. Crushing the fresh response is considered good planning necessary to keep everything on track. The "dress rehearsals" for board of directors' meetings are a classic example. The reasons given are, "We don't want to waste their time" and "We have to appear as professional and planned as possible." The reality is that the last thing we want is for the directors to know the whole complex, stirring brew that is the real organization. If you are ever on a board, push to eliminate the preplanning overkill, and fight to get some fresh people and perspective into the room. Find out if anyone in the organization really *cares* about all this stuff. Spontaneity is annoying. We need to deliberately create forums for maximum annoyance.

Build Bureaucracy

Bureaucracy is "management or administration marked by diffusion of authority among numerous offices and adherence to inflexible rules of operation. . . . An administrative system in which the need or inclination to follow complex procedures impedes effective action."[3] Bureaucracies often develop from rational thought, but their inflexibility and obsession with complex procedures lead straight to irrationality. The driving passion can become how to beat the system. All procedures and rules should have to justify their existence at least annually.

Misuse Negative Passion

People are really frustrated and angry, and they are letting it be known. But at least there is *passion*. It may be negative, but it's something. We have some raw material to work with. We need to separate the destroyers from those who are upset because we are being less than we can be, and then listen to the latter group. We can involve them in changing the things they so passionately hate. We won't be able to find anyone who cares more about the problem than someone who has attacked it relentlessly with the intent to make it better.

Promote the Wrong People

Nothing so clearly states the values of the organization as the act of promoting. We say we value respect, and then we promote a person who degrades people. Just *having* a boss is often passion-crunching enough. When the boss is rotten to boot, send passion to the emergency room.

Be Callous

We move people around like pawns on a chessboard. They have no control over what they work on, where they work on it, or whom they work on it with. Or, we treat people like cargo, and toss them overboard when the seas get rough. It's hard to be passionate in a war when your buddies and other innocents are getting shot by your own officers.

Mumble

Absence of clear, two-way communication is very frustrating and passion-debilitating. We need to open our system up to the whole

range of communication: the loud, the brassy, the obnoxious, the dis-
agreeable, the contrarian—whatever will allow the fires to burn. All
of our communication, whether verbal, written, intranet, one-on-one,
or with a group, needs to leave people more passionate—or it needs
to be abandoned.

Put Them to Sleep

There is a push in many quarters to make the workplace more
comfortable. But comfort tends to relax human beings and put them
to sleep. We have to work on giving people pleasure (waking people
up) rather than giving them comfort (putting people to sleep). We
need to find practical ways to build pleasure and stimulate people,
and ways to minimize comfort and prevent them from nodding off.

Conclusion

We cannot treat people in these ways and expect them to care and
work passionately for our organizations. As Tom Brown says, "When
work becomes meaningless, when corporations don't incorporate
people with purpose, when the future seems to be both threatening
and a mirage, then little is left but one's ability to laugh at caustic car-
toons or billboard posters—and to doubt."[4]

What if we realize that our organization is dispassionate as a
whole? What if we're full of people who have no passion? Is there any
hope? Yes, there is. We have a chance to see fire if we remove the obstacles, at least from those who are properly matched. Those who
aren't matched and can't be will have to leave, as will those who are
passionless and won't choose to come back to life. So often I'm asked
in a seminar, "Why don't they care?" So often, the answer is painfully
simple: *Because they don't care.*

The question for the passionless is, "What would it take to see
you resurrect?" Put it to them. Our job isn't to create passion, it's simply to find it and unleash it. If people have no viable answer, we can't
help them. And they can't help us.

There are a lot of ways for passion to appear, and we can and
should evaluate them. And there are a lot of things we can do to kill
passion, and we can and should stop doing them.

Passion, first and foremost.

Notes

1. As quoted in Robert McGarvey, "Get Psyched," *Entrepreneur,* May 1994, p. 84.
2. Robert D. Kaplan, "Travels into America's Future," *The Atlantic Monthly,* August 1998, p. 42.
3. *The American Heritage Dictionary of the English Language, Third Edition* (Boston: Houghton Mifflin Company, 1996).
4. Thomas L. Brown, *The Anatomy of Fire* (www.mgeneral.com), 1997.

15

Deal With Negative and Missing Passion

The best lack all conviction, while the worst
Are full of passionate intensity.

—W. B. Yeats, "The Second Coming"

Whenever we confront an unbridled desire we are surely in the
presence of a tragedy-in-the-making.

—Quentin Crisp, *Manners From Heaven*

The line separating good and evil passes not through states,
nor between political parties either—but right through every
human heart.

—Aleksandr Solzhenitsyn, *The Gulag Archipelago*

One of the realities of life is that most people are passionate about something, even if it's just gossiping. Passion, in and of itself, is not a cure-all, or even a good thing. At its worst, it can devour our organizations.

Negative passion comes in a number of guises: the Shadow, the Petty, the Indignant, and the True Believer.

Let's look at each of these in turn.

The Shadow

Passions can be driven by the best that is in us, or by the shadow.

We can walk an elderly person across the street, and then rage and scream and honk at the elderly person driving so slowly down the street. We can be fired up to lose some weight, and then enthusiastically gorge ourselves on some irresistible chocolate. We can give a moving speech about how it will take "all of us" to achieve certain goals, and then participate in a scathing, behind-doors session that dissects and degrades the very same people.

There are many less than nice things inside of us that can drive unhelpful and even destructive passions. Hatred is a monstrously destructive organizational force, but if we aren't willing to acknowledge its existence, we can close our eyes and refuse to rid ourselves of nasty people and abusive managers. Jealousy and envy can cripple our efforts to be competitive externally, but if we aren't willing to root them out, we will have people holding back top subordinates or building fiefdoms at the organization's expense.[1]

The shadow can be very hard to detect at times. People who fundamentally disrespect our authority, for example, can claim to follow our leadership and insist that others do likewise, as long as they like what we're doing. But when we start moving in a legitimate direction that they don't like, it will become clear that they recognize no authority but their own.

These negative passions can eat up an organization from the inside out. We can't afford to illude that they don't exist, or that their effects will not be ugly.

- Negative passion can turn someone into an Attila: "Nothing grows where he has been." An organizational Attila may harass or fire the best achievers because they *are* the best achievers. Some people are uncomfortable with achievement and work to tear it down by attacking, nitpicking, and boxing people in. They especially hate those who appear to threaten their stranglehold on power.

- Negative passion can cause people to turn their department or office or plant into a Viking ship and other groups into smoldering ruins. They use projects and meetings as opportunities to show up other groups. They assign the poorest performers to work with disliked departments and teams, regardless of the damage to the overall organization. They fight for "booty"—for example, the biggest budget increases—even if the money would be better spent elsewhere.

- Negative passion can even turn enemies into "friends," as when Hitler and Stalin agreed to carve up Europe. People who have battled one another can suddenly turn into collaborators when they see an opportunity to increase their power or to destroy a person or idea that threatens their current preeminence.

The problem isn't just that negative passions are in and of themselves destructive. They also destroy any possibility of positive passion. It is practically impossible, for example, to be constructively passionate in an environment of fear and criticism. People who have a passion to hurt or use other people can follow a "scorched earth" policy, where nothing good is allowed to grow.

We should never underestimate the negative passions that emerge from the shadow. They can't be reformed; they can only be contained or eliminated. Too few writers, speakers, consultants, and academicians are willing to acknowledge the presence of evil, in ourselves or in others. Ignoring it doesn't make it go away; rather, it gives the shadow room to grow and destroy. These negative passions must be accounted for, hemmed in, excised, and wiped out. And we have to be vigilant to make sure it happens.

Finally, we have to remember that these negative passions exist inside of *people*. Actual, real, breathing people. When something terrible happens, when something destructive occurs within our organization, we can rest assured that there is someone, or a group of someones, behind it. Only dealing with those people, clearly and quickly and forcefully—and with an even greater amount of passion—will solve the problem. They are "infinitely implacable, because there was no reasoning with dead souls.[2]

The rational organization is particularly vulnerable to the shadow because it says that nonrational factors don't matter and discounts their influence. It resists making value judgments like "good versus bad" and "right versus wrong." Ignoring people's hearts gives the shadow room to grow. I watched a large corporation reassign one evil person over and over, under the rational concepts that "we just haven't found his niche" and "it's just a failure to communicate." He left wreckage everywhere.

The Petty

An offshoot of the shadow, but perhaps not quite as destructive to the organization, is the pettiness that permeates daily life.

Tyrants commit murder, even genocide. They use guns and secret police to control people. Terror is their greatest weapon.

Petty tyrants are not nearly so grandiose. They don't kill people, but they kill flow and initiative. They don't use guns and secret police, but they wield thick manuals and rules and "the system" to control and flatten others. They don't use terror, but they leave a great mark with their greatest weapon: nitpicking.

Petty tyrants usually have passion, but it is only for themselves or for their own area of responsibility (or at least control). They often do it to puff up their own importance, to make themselves feel powerful at another's expense. Sometimes they do it just because it can be done.

It isn't that they don't know that this is a life-draining approach. It's that they don't care. Their petty business, their way, their rules, their procedures are all-important. Everything else has to fall into line. An old proverb says, "It is all right to be zealous, as long as the purpose is good." Petty tyrants have no good purpose, and so we can't let their zeal eat away the soul of our organization.

The worst part of these petty tyrants is that they're hell-bent on reproducing themselves. They will go to the ends of the earth to win a convert to their "cause" of politics and micromanagement, and then work to make that convert into an even pettier tyrant—someone who is even more of a tyrant, and even pettier.

This conclave of petty tyrants eats away at people's confidence and sense of value. An ancient proverb says that if a ruler listens to lies, all of his officials will become liars. These people are centers of ruinous gossip, as they enjoy listening to dirt about employees and encourage people to tattle on each other. When pettiness is on the throne, gossip becomes the currency of the kingdom.

The Indignant

A number of things that happen in organizational life can produce negative passions that are expressed in the form of righteous indignation. It isn't necessarily bad that people are reacting negatively to a negative stimulus; however, their response, if left unattended, is still counterproductive to organizational life.

A word of caution is needed. We're not talking here about disagreement or dissent arising from unjust organizational actions. Disagreement of that nature isn't negative passion, but rather a response to unfairness. If the organization is wrong, the organization needs to change. Otherwise we'll give the dictators among us the excuse to ruthlessly suppress all dissent under the guise of crushing negative passion.

Let's take a look at some of the most common causes of indignation, and offer some suggestions for curing them.

• *Personal values misaligned with the organization's values.* If people don't really believe in our values, it is only natural that they will be feisty about them, disagree with them, refuse to practice them, be annoyed by them. Over time, they will work either to change the organization's values or to sabotage them. We can't afford either approach, even from very talented people. We're not likely to change our deeply held organizational values; if these people believe in the "lone ranger" approach and we preach collaboration, for example, we're not likely to get them to become what to them would be cogs in a machine. We have to ferret out this mismatch at the beginning or as soon as possible thereafter. If the problem is sabotage, we have to take dramatic action or our organization's life will be cannibalized.

• *Decisions based on illusion rather than reality.* When people think we're making irrational decisions, they will find it difficult or impossible to support these decisions, and are more likely to work for their downfall. It may be that they just don't see the whole reality; in that case, we need to do more explaining. For example, if we are closing down an office or plant whose product line is widely perceived to be profitable or a key to offering full service, without a lot of communication and opportunity to get questions answered, people will assume the worst about the intelligence of the leadership. Of course, if we really *are* making decisions based on illusions, we will always drive good people into opposition and rebellion. We have to confront reality and act on what we see—continuously.

• *Perception that the organization has dealt with people in a hypocritical or unfair manner.* Justice and fairness are defined a bit differently in different cultures, but they are very important to us as human beings, regardless of culture. Fairness is one of the first and most intensely held values exhibited by children. My own reaction, when I have seen someone unjustly punished or terminated, is to lose respect for the organization and to become a spokesperson for the downtrodden. Once again, if the action *was* honest and fair, perhaps we haven't been open enough so that people know it. If we really are arbitrary with people, well . . .

• *Control and heavy-handedness.* People and cultures have different tolerance levels for being controlled and manipulated, but most people don't like it. Control is an illusion—we can't even control whether we will be alive tomorrow, so how can we control complex human beings and organizations? Control is sometimes benign (driven by misunderstanding) and sometimes malignant (driven by dysfunction). But it is always a dispiriting force. We will deal with this in much more depth in the next chapter.

• *Absence of rights, due process, and a court of appeal.* It is unbelievable that many organizations don't have mechanisms for dealing with abuse of human and organizational rights. To be sure, there are rules against discrimination based on all sorts of criteria, and there are mechanisms to enforce health and safety issues. But what about the most ordinary abuses? What about the supervisor who just treats a subordinate like dirt, without crossing any legal lines? No intelligent person would want to live in a country that didn't have a means of redress. Organizations, if they are serious about eliminating negative passions, can't ignore this critical need. Mechanisms could include open access outside the chain of command, an ombudsman, or a review board that includes a good cross section of people.

• *Dealing with people as a human "resource" rather than as complex individual beings.* One of the most loathsome terms created in recent years is *human resource.* It's even worse than *personnel.* It takes the most dignified and noble being on the planet—an individual person—and reduces him or her to the status of a resource. And it isn't even *that* good, because we call people "resources" and then don't treat them that way. Enhancement of equipment is an investment; enhancement of a person (learning, development) is an expense. This is the logical extreme of the rational, mechanistic approach, the victory of head over heart. People are just another resource; let's plan and label and categorize and plug them in and optimize. No wonder people get angry about this. We should never underestimate anyone.

• *Existence of an "us versus them" mentality.* This is often created by internal, win-lose competition between people (like salespeople), departments, or divisions. If the organization is to thrive, everyone has to realize that "them" is "us." We have to eliminate the internal, dog-eat-dog competition inside of the organization. According to the

Chicago Tribune, when Motorola recently announced the elimination of 15,000 jobs worldwide, one of the major reasons given was a "warring tribes" culture that encouraged divisions and departments within the company to compete against one another. We can minimize these negative passions by focusing attention on *external* us-versus-them competition. In other words, we have to learn how to cooperate internally so that we can compete ferociously externally. This means that we give up all programs and practices (such as sales competitions and employee-of-the-month awards) that pit us against one another rather than against the real enemy. Do we need to cooperate or compete? Yes. Just in different places.

 • *Incompetent leaders and coworkers.* Having a passionate organization doesn't mean tolerating poor performers—even if they *are* enthusiastic. Incompetence in leaders rightly drives people crazy, and ultimately inflames their anger if we don't correct the problem. And often, when some workers are incompetent, their competent coworkers end up carrying the ball—probably without getting the credit, but probably getting the blame. One manager I knew would yell at the accounting people for incomplete sales data, when it was the salespeople who were negligent in turning in their paperwork accurately and on time.

 • *Dishonesty.* Dishonesty is a phenomenal breeder of indignation. Organizations can convey dishonesty both in what they say ("This is what we're thinking about"—the old trial balloon) and in what they don't say (at Hallmark, for example, there was a built-in reluctance to share bad news). And people are pretty savvy; they'll pick most of this up. Trust in and respect for the organization evaporate. Even *lavish* communication isn't as important as *honest* communication.

In the case of righteous indignation, negative passion is at least better than no passion. At least there is still life out there. But we have to transform or eliminate these passions without delay by honestly evaluating and effectively responding to the source of the indignation. If left unaddressed, these feelings are a waste of passion, time, and resources, and a distraction from what we are trying to accomplish.

The True Believer

This source of negative passion comes from the collision of two positive passions.

Two people can be equally passionate about two different and opposing ideas. This is not a personality conflict (although that could add to the problem). These are two passionate people butting heads over ideas in which they truly believe—but only one of which can "win."

One high-tech business I led had capability in several diverse areas, including medical devices and aerospace. On the aerospace side, two of my key people entered a protracted war over whether we should allocate resources to the government/military sector or the private sector. They both believed they were right, and both were very persuasive.

At an initial level, this can be a wonderful situation. As we discussed in Chapter 10, this constructive conflict or creative abrasion can help hone both ideas and move the entire organization to a higher plane. We *want* people to care about their ideas and projects, we *want* them to be champions, we *want* them to stand up and fight for what they believe.

But we can't let the conflict go on forever, or it will destroy two good people, two good ideas, and maybe the fire in our organization. The combatants can become obsessed with proving themselves right and the other wrong. Both ideas can be decimated, and the "winner" sabotaged by the "loser." A lot of collateral damage can be caused while the war is being waged.

In mathematical terms, two negatives make a positive. In this case, two positives can make a negative.

We have to have some mechanisms in place—preferably in advance—to defuse the situation. Perhaps it is an arbitration, with you as the arbitrator. We don't want to have the two parties restate their cases—that will only entrench them further and make them more intractable. And we want to eliminate the "win-lose" atmosphere—the best negotiations are those from which everyone goes away a little bit unhappy. This is what I did with the aerospace "war": We agreed to drop our routine manufacturing in both sectors and to expand work in both areas that could build on our recognized high-quality system. Another approach would be to give the party who didn't sell her or his idea the responsibility for implementing a juicy part of the "winner," so that she or he gets a chunk of the credit. It's even better if that juicy part resembles at least a portion of the original, "losing" idea.

Whatever else we do, we know we want some lions working for us. We just don't want them to devour each other.

Can Positive Passion Ever Be Wrong?

Is it possible that people, consciously or otherwise, could obscure a necessary, objective, rational truth about a situation?

Yes.

An efficient, well-run, enthusiastic plant is making a product that can no longer be sold at a profit. It's our least troublesome operation, and we like all the people. We're passionate about it. Could this cloud our rational judgment? Absolutely.

Passion is not a substitute for thought. Sometimes, when the numbers are guesses, mere extrapolations, or worst-case scenarios, passion has to override. But when the facts are clear, when the numbers and analysis are no longer undeniable, passion needs to yield.

This really isn't the setting aside of passion, or a case of letting reason rule. In reality, we are replacing a passion for a project or direction with a passion for truth.

Conclusion

Passions come in two flavors: positive and negative.

Convert the negative if you can.

But don't underestimate it.

Notes

1. For a full treatment of the horrible but ordinary uses some people can make of power, and some practical solutions, see my book *Balance of Power* (New York: AMACOM, 1997), especially Chapter 12, "Destructive Power," Chapter 14, "Keeping Power Out of the Wrong Hands," and Chapter 17, "Conquering the Factors That Breed Destructive Power."
2. Robert Stone, *Damascus Gate* (New York: Houghton Mifflin Company, 1998), p. 302.

16

Kill the Concept of "Management"

You cannot manage men into battle. You manage things; you lead people.

—Grace Murray Hopper, admiral, U.S. Navy (retired)

As for the best leaders, the people do not notice their existence. The next best, the people honor and praise. The next, the people fear; and the next, the people hate.

—Lao-Tzu, *Tao Te Ching*

When times get tough, old established businesses with managers but no leaders seek help.

—David J. Morris, Jr., *Performance and Instruction Journal*

We can lead passion, or we can manage lethargy.

Leaders are not born, any more than violinists are. Some people may have a natural talent for playing the violin, but they will never become violinists unless and until they learn how to play. The rest of us will never be maestros, but we still have some kind of music in our souls. We enjoy it, listen to it, sing along with it, and can learn to perform it. We may not be able to play first violin, but we can still be in the orchestra.

And so it is with leadership. Some may have a talent for it and, if they work at it, become great leaders, the "first violinists" of organizations. But most of the rest of us have some kind of leadership in our souls. We can learn how to lead, do it, and even enjoy it. We may be mentoring one other human being while the great leader leads 10,000, but we are leaders nonetheless.

To lead another person, all we need is some education in leadership, the desire to lead, and that person's passion about where we are leading him or her.

But management is a different animal.

Management—planning, organizing, directing, and controlling—is the vestigial legacy of scientific management and a much simpler marketplace. In practice, it's even worse; organizational expert Peter Drucker has said that 85 percent of management consists of putting obstacles in people's way. Drucker says, "I'm not comfortable with the word *manager* anymore, because it implies subordinates."[1]

Management is a sure-fire way to squash passion and emotion. People can't be managed, and today many of the best people *won't* be managed. I heard one management expert say, "You need only three things to manage people: a policy manual, job descriptions, and performance evaluations." Makes organizations sound sort of like an obedience school for dogs, doesn't it?

It's even worse. Organizations are *layered* obedience schools. We hire workers, who are watched by supervisors, who are watched by department managers, who are watched by division managers. The focus is top down, with a ton of non-value-adding watching going on. Either we have too many layers of "management" or we have really stupid people.

Now, some organizations have found a way to have both. They have all the layers, and they have treated people like nincompoops for so long that their employees have *become* nincompoops. The organization's whole focus is on those inept, untrustworthy minions at the bottom of all that watching. To become a manager in many organizations is to opt for a career in babysitting.

The real vision is to unleash all employees as leaders, and to turn the organization's focus into adding value for customers and other stakeholders.

In other words, management focuses down and in, while leadership—at all levels—focuses up and out.

In this chapter we will explore the demise of the management paradigm, and the need for an organization to hasten that demise if it wants to be a passionate organization.

The Illusion of Management

To *manage* is "to direct or control the use of; handle. . . . To exert control over. . . . To make submissive to one's authority, discipline, or persuasion."[2]

Let's tackle these definitions one at a time.

"To direct or control the use of" says that the traditional management functions of planning, organizing, directing, and controlling are performed by one person while the actual work is done by another. The first illusion implied in this definition is that we can separate the planning and coordinating of the work from the doing of it. This is the philosophy of the old assembly line, and even there it usually doesn't work as well as other approaches. "Direct and control" presumes that a few do the thinking and the many do the now-mindless labor. The deficiency of this assumption is summed up in the lament of a pioneer of assembly lines, Henry Ford: "How come when I want a pair of hands I get a human being as well?" This has almost always been a less-than-optimum way to deal with complex human beings; in an age of exploding knowledge and knowledge workers, and very different expectations, it is a fatal illusion.

Part of this first definition is to "handle"—the word *manage* itself comes from a root that implies getting our hands onto something. We can handle a project. But how on earth do we handle a human being? There is simply no way.

The second definition takes us even further into illusion: "to exert control over." We can't even guarantee that people will show up tomorrow, much less that they will work at their best, be creative and innovative, and worry in their spare time about how they can make a difference for our organization. How can we exert control over people in a free society? It isn't easy even in an unfree society; only the most horrible totalitarian states and despicable dictators manage it at all. And even the worst of these end up with black markets and underground movements.

The third definition is "to make submissive to one's authority, discipline, or persuasion." To make someone submissive is to bend that person's will and push it down, under our own. It says, "I'm on top and you're not." It relies on policy and procedures manuals and their corresponding discipline. "Persuasion" is the only part of this definition that approximates leadership. But if we are operating under the illusion of management, we won't bother with persuasion for very long. In truth, we persuade only because they're afraid.

The Problems of Management

The first problem with management is that we apply the concept to other people.

Management is a necessary function, but it is necessary *as it relates to our own work.* It is fruitless to try to manage anyone else. Why?

• No one wants to be managed. In decades of consulting to and working in organizations, I have never heard anyone say, "I need to be managed more." But they say all the time that they need to be *led* more.

• Any intelligent person will resent being managed. Management is an insulting concept—no competent person needs or wants to be managed in her or his daily life. People make huge decisions about education, career, family, friends, financial issues, and a host of other big-ticket issues without being managed or controlled.

• We simply can't be there enough to really manage even a few people. If the burden is on us to keep people from messing up, we will have to be all over them all the time. But management is like bad parenting: We treat people like children, and then we're surprised that they *act* that way. Great parents *lead* their children; they treat them like they want them to become—with dignity, respect, guidance, and personal example. Ultimately, anyone who needs to be managed needs to be fired.

• Management sets up self-inhibiting and self-destructive boundaries. It is limiting rather than expansive. It focuses on the "one best way" (there is none) and all the things a person shouldn't do (the longer the list of rules, the more we direct people's creativity to finding ways around them).

• The very concept of management creates a host of unhelpful assumptions: I have to spend a lot of my time managing people; People need to be managed; Without my direction this organization will slack off or come apart. It leads to lots of time and energy to think up rules and controls (obstacles). It wastes a lot of time and energy (telling, monitoring, and reporting). And it can produce rebellion, disempowerment, and demandingness ("You're there, so help!") all at the same time.

• Management creates divisions. Thinking at the top and doing at the bottom is fundamentally disempowering. Creating a system of "watchers" and "watchees" is fundamentally alienating. The manager, in a destructive but inexorable process, becomes the customer as people's focus is split.

There is a second problem: We have been taught that leading and managing are done by separate *people* ("managers" and "leaders"), when they are really separate *functions*. Almost every person is called upon to lead others in some fashion, and we all have to manage our own work. The question, "Who are the leaders and who are the managers?" is a pointless academic exercise. The critical question is, "How do we get all of our people to effectively lead others and efficiently manage their own work?"[3]

Management is the last refuge of a bad leader. It is the red herring of leadership. In its worst form, micromanagement, leadership is abandoned and the rules become everything.

And micromanagement is exacerbated by a third problem: Many people bring their own ideas about their own freedom (or lack thereof) to the table. Management can turn even very capable people into drones. A true leader finds that many people don't respond positively to the offer of freedom and responsibility; they've never experienced it, are afraid of it, and don't want it. As R. Alec Mackenzie points out in *The Time Trap*, "A boss's mere expression of an opinion can be interpreted as a decision—even a direct order—by a staff member caught in the clutches of risk avoidance." Only by countering this reluctance and fear with a massive reeducation program will freedom be given the chance to really work. Russians and people in the former Soviet states have found that there is a huge difference between having freedom and knowing what to do with it.

A fourth problem is that management is more likely to stifle growth (personal or organizational) than it is to enhance it. Management is inherently static—it busies itself with taking what is and making it more productive or efficient. It is a caretaker function. At its worst, this caretaking approach keeps us from abandoning losing or non-value-adding activities—after all, our job isn't to challenge these activities, attack these activities, or laugh at these activities; our job is to *manage* them, to make them more efficient. Management can't think out of the box because its job is to take care of the box.

And this leads to the fifth and biggest problem of all with management: Management can never lead to passion. Never. It can squelch passion, but it can't enlarge it or even keep it alive. Managers don't want face-to-face contact; detailed reports are more efficient. Forget "management by walking around"; if you have a problem, you can send a memo, which is more productive. Managers want order, calmness, the quiet hum of a well-maintained piece of machinery. Passion is loud, brassy, and very uncalm. Not only can management never lead to passion, it may be passion's most organized enemy.

Killing the Concept of Management

If we believe the time has come to abandon this leftover of a different world, there are some steps we can take to kill the concept of management:

  • We can realize that we can't reform a top-down hierarchy. The system (the philosophy of organizational life and design) is fundamentally flawed. It is structured to think at the top and work at the bottom. It separates decision making from implementation. It calls people at the top "leaders," people in the middle "managers," and people at the bottom "workers." It can't and won't reform itself; it is on an irreversible course and cannot be reformed, but only replaced. It needs to be blown up and rebuilt. Reengineering won't save us from this flaw that is so fatal in a time of such great change.

  • We can adopt powersharing as our modus operandi. Power sharing is different from empowerment. Empowerment says, "I have the power, and I will grant some of it to you," whereas power sharing says, "We all bring power to the table—the power to create, to destroy, to accomplish, to do nothing—so how do we bring out the best and eliminate the worst? And what is the best mix for this project, this mission, this season?" Empowerment is a real improvement over management, but it is only a halfway house. (The differences are highlighted in Table 16-1.) The case can be made that the failure of entire nations is often traceable to an unwillingness to powershare, rather than to problems of climate, geography, or natural resources. The tragic story of Africa, for example, revolves around the steadfast refusal of the tribes that make up so many of the nations to share power with one another and transfer it peacefully. How can our organizations win in the twenty-first century if we make the same mistake?[4]

• We can take immediate steps to reduce and eliminate unnecessary (read: most) policies, procedures, job descriptions, etc. "Leaders ... work to create positive emotional energy in others ... by structuring the organization to get rid of bureaucratic nonsense."[5] We must struggle to create an environment in which leaders can take root and grow at every level.

• We can replace policy manuals with agreed-upon vision and values, procedures manuals with descriptions of appropriate behaviors, job descriptions with ownership, performance evaluations with performance agreements and self-selected projects, and most reporting with trust.

• We can move away from doing things *to* and *for* people and toward joint progress. "The leader can replace training with development," John Hughes, president of Creative Leadership Strategies, told me. "Training is something we do *to* people; development is something we do *with* them." The adult-child paradigm simply has to be eliminated.

• We can focus on purpose and values rather than on structure. Who we are and why we are here is more important than how we are supposed to fit into an organizational hierarchy. Once we have found passionate people, we need to fit the organization to the people rather than the people to the organization. We need to let the organizational design follow the needs of our human capital and our needs for information and knowledge.

• We can kill hierarchy by getting everyone wrapped up in critical, time-sensitive missions, projects, and goals. Someone who is drowning doesn't care who rescues her or him. If people aren't on their toes with value-adding stuff, they will be on one another's toes with value-subtracting stuff.

• We can plan for passion. We can use planning as a "dreaming" function first and a synthesizing function second, rather than as an extrapolating function first and a dissecting function second. We can evaluate our organizational future and its many scenarios on the passion scale: How much do we care about this idea? How many of us care about it? Do we have enough fire to get it over the top? Planning needs to be soft and flexible and porous, rather than the usual hard and rigid and impenetrable.

Table 16-1   Differences Between Management, Empowerment, and Powersharing

Management	Empowerment	Powersharing
As dictators: Power is hoarded at the top.	*As kings:* Power is accumulated and granted by fiat or charter.	*As equals:* Power is coaxed onto the table from all parties.
Solid: Power is stored in blocks at headquarters.	*Fluid:* Power is transferred or diverted to positions, departments, or projects.	*Gas:* Power is everywhere it is needed or can produce value.
Inheritance: We have served the "family," and it belongs to us.	*Limited quantity:* There is only so much power; giving it to others diminishes our own.	*Expansive:* Power is contagious; if your power grows, so do mine and ours.
Diamonds: Power is beautiful, and we look good in it.	*Gold:* Power is hard to get, and we will be cautious in giving it away.	*Commodity:* Power is generally available throughout the organization.
Treasure: We keep it in the safe.	*Treat:* We keep it over their heads.	*Tool:* We keep it handy.
Monopoly: Power belongs by title to certain people.	*Crony capitalism:* Power is given to the favored few.	*Free market:* Power belongs by right to everyone who enters the game.

• We can transform our whole idea of planning, making it a position of advocacy for change rather than a defender of the status quo.

• We can teach our leaders to vary their leadership style. One size doesn't fit all. People are too complex. Some situations need direction; some need protection. Some people need prodding; some simply need a sounding board. We need to understand a key principle of leadership: *It isn't leadership if the followers don't get it.*

Management is a sickness when applied to other people.
We need to kill it before it kills us.

The Advantages of Leadership for the Passionate Organization

We have discussed the problems with management as traditionally practiced and how to address them. The advantages of adapting the self-management, leadership-at-all-levels paradigm, particularly for increasing passion, are given in Table 16-2.

Table 16-2   Advantages of Leadership at All Levels

Issue	Management	Leadership
Authority	It's mine.	It's yours.
Responsibility	It's yours.	It's ours.
Accountability	I'm watching.	We're watching.
Communication	One-way.	Multidimensional
Learning	I'll decide.	You choose.
Ideas	I'll evaluate them.	You develop them.
Innovations	I'll approve them.	Do them.
Quality	I'll measure.	You monitor.

Table 16-2   (continued)

Goals	I'll determine.	We'll agree.
Priorities	I'll set.	You set.
Budgets	Control	Self-management
Motivation	It's my job.	It's your life.

Conclusion

The game has changed entirely when we've killed the concept of management. People are free with much expected of them, rather than controlled with much demanded of them.

Once it's really our baby—to bear, to nurture, to care for, to bring to maturity—our passion can and will flourish. Even while we might dread babysitting a relatively calm and quiet child that is not our own, we think nothing about staying awake through the night with our own sick or frightened child. By the fact that we are human, we treasure that which is our own, and feel passion for it that no reason can explain.

Notes

1. Peter F. Drucker, *Managing in a Time of Great Change* (New York: Truman Talley Books, 1995), p. 17.
2. From *The American Heritage Dictionary of the English Language, Third Edition* (New York: Houghton Mifflin Company, 1996).
3. For a more complete treatment of the leader versus manager issue, see my book *Balance of Power* (New York: AMACOM, 1998), especially pp. 28–29, 96–98, and 101–102.
4. Power sharing is one of the key themes in *Balance of Power*. The book covers such critical topics as the myths of power, powersharing requirements and methods, steps in balancing the quality of power, constructive and destructive power, critical traits of the power-worthy, and keeping power out of the wrong hands.
5. Noel M. Tichy, *The Leadership Engine* (New York: HarperBusiness, 1997), p. 20.

17

Know It's Better to Stub Your Toe Than to Lose Your Leg

No passion so effectually robs the mind of all its powers of acting and reasoning as fear.

—Edmund Burke, *The Origin of our Ideas of the Sublime and Beautiful*

Failure is good. It's fertilizer. Everything I've learned about coaching I've learned from making mistakes.

—Rick Pitino, professional basketball coach

Everywhere you trip is where the treasure lies.

—Norman Lear, television producer

The fear of making mistakes—of stubbing our organizational toe—will have to be finally destroyed in the successful organization of the future. Passion will lead to some injuries, perhaps even some serious pain, but it will usually prevent major amputations and death.

This willingness to stub toes in order to avoid amputations means that we need to have some key ingredients in place in our culture: creativity at the core, an acceptance (and even embracing) of the mavericks who create, an environment in which it is safe for everyone (not just mavericks) to take risks, and an appreciation for the role that short-term pain (from failure and mistakes) can have in preparing us for a mobile future.

Let's look at each of these ingredients in turn.

Creativity at the Core

The essence of growth, the quintessential aspect of it, is creativity. Creativity is the process of taking a number of ideas or principles or facts that already exist, and combining them in a new way to bring something different into existence. There is no way to grow in the long term without creativity, and yet most organizations are woefully inadequate environments for fostering it.

Although the brew that produces creativity is complex, a number of key ingredients are necessary if creativity is to emerge:

• *Freedom.* First and foremost, people need to be free (not just to feel free) for their minds to be able to *play*, which is the level we have to reach if we are going to create value. People must be free to think for themselves, express their ideas and doubts, associate with those of their own choosing, disagree with ideas no matter how deeply entrenched, and question everything. As we step down from freedom, we step down from creativity.

• *Access.* People must have access to all sorts of information, knowledge, ideas, and even half-baked concepts. Limited pools of data produce only extrapolations of current directions into the future. We just don't know enough to break out. We have to understand the reality that "there are more things in heaven and earth . . . than are dreamt of in your philosophy."[1]

• *Both/and thinking.* Leaders must create an environment in which people think in terms of "both/and" rather than "either/or." Either/or thinking is limiting and can even be destructive, especially when both choices seem to be bad ("We can either lay off 20 percent of the workforce or cancel our planned capital expansion program"). We need to encourage expansiveness, not limitations, in people's thought processes.

• *Welcoming complexity.* When we put on our managers' hats, we strive to reduce and eliminate complexity, to get down to the core, to "stick to our knitting." But when we think clearly, as leaders, we see that the world is a very complex place, and that our current understandings and presuppositions are always only an approximation of reality. At times, we have to admit that they are a very poor approximation, if indeed they relate to reality at all.

• *Diversity.* People must have many sources of ideas and challenges to existing ideas, whether they think they want the diversity that produces this or not. Diversity can include different personality types, the young and old, new and experienced, synthesizers and analyzers, artists and craftsmen, male and female, different cultural backgrounds, different educational and work history, and different passions. Organizations that resist diversity of souls and passions will shrivel and die in the new economy; those that accept diversity as the "right" and "proper" and "legal" thing to do may be able to survive at some level; but those that welcome total diversity, thrive on it, love it, and maximize its presence will conquer. Promoting diversity as a legal requirement is the lowest life form, the amoeba of organizational life. Welcoming diversity is organizational development at the highest level.

• *Seed casting.* The organization and all its components (divisions, departments, plants, stores, teams, natural work groups, individuals) must be oriented toward casting seeds. An ancient proverb tells us, "Sow your seed in the morning, and at evening let not your hands be idle, for you do not know which will succeed, whether this or that, or whether both will do equally well."[2] This is the "try a lot of stuff and keep what works" approach. In practice, this means that our people have to be able and willing to pursue any idea that could be fruitful, at least to the extent of finding out that it is a dead end. The alternative is to "keep doing the same stuff and hope it keeps working."

• *Mistake-friendly.* We have to lose our aversion to mistakes. "An essential aspect of creativity is not being afraid to fail," said Edwin Land, the inventor of the Polaroid camera. I have seen leader after leader preach this truth, but few live it. When the mistake costs us money or time or opportunity or customers (and all mistakes are going to cost one or more of these), it's hard to remember our preaching and easy to be annoyed. Our first response to the mistake is the key; it sets the tone. If it is even slightly less than positive and understanding and enthusiastic and celebratory, it's all over. The number of "tries" will shrink to the minimum necessary to keep the job. This also means that we have to rid ourselves of those who punish people for honest mistakes. Speaking of his invention of the light bulb, Thomas Edison said, "I have not failed. I've just found 10,000 ways that don't work."

If we do these things, we can encourage a passion for creativity and the growth derived from it.

Mavericks Matter

If we happen to have the good fortune to come across a constructive maverick, we should do everything we can to hire and keep that person.

A maverick is someone who "refuses to abide by the dictates of or resists adherence to a group; a dissenter." To be a maverick is to be "independent in thought and action or exhibiting such independence."[3]

Mavericks can be either good or bad, constructive or destructive. Destructive mavericks cannot be tolerated if the organization is to survive, let alone thrive. Their devotion is to their own path, their own way—even to the destruction (if necessary) of the group. They dissent when it would be easier to assent, disagree when it would be to their advantage to agree, and violate group norms even when the group is behaving in a way that pleases them.

Constructive mavericks, on the other hand, are worth their weight in gold. They won't just go along under the false banner of "cooperation." They won't be team players when the team is being slaughtered or is playing the wrong game. Their first thought is, "What are we missing here?" rather than, "Gee, it's really wonderful that we're all getting along so well." They sound alarms, raise concerns, and disagree with stupidity. They can be feisty, ornery, and downright obnoxious. But they aren't doing it for their personal agenda or to destroy the group, they are doing it for the betterment of the group. "Disruptive people are an asset," says retired Chrysler vice chairman Bob Lutz. "They're the irritating grains of sand that, in the case of oysters, every now and then produce a pearl."[4]

Of course, every obnoxious person thinks that this is her or his motivation, so how do we know when it's really true? How do we think about someone who continues to fight over every detail of a new direction? It is a question of both motivation and scale. Is the motivation to make it better, or to make a point? Can the person tell the difference in scale between a linchpin issue that should never be compromised and an important issue on which he or she could yield?

The best possible organization would be a team of mavericks. The concepts seem mutually exclusive. How can they be a team if they're a bunch of independents? How can people who go their own way make up any kind of team? Hollywood consistently makes this happen. The key is the vision and the values. If these mavericks are heading toward a common and important destination, they will fight and claw and argue, but they will push each other toward the finish line. I have built teams like this. It can be scary, but it has always been fun. I can't think of anything more likely to bring passion to the surface than to build this kind of team, a nonteam team, an ungroupable group, a collection of absolutely unique-and-glad-of-it individuals.

Most organizations, obviously, don't do this. In fact, the press is usually on to kill mavericks and drive maverick behavior out of the organization. This effort is fueled by control and fear. Organizations that are bent on control cannot abide mavericks, because mavericks by their very nature won't be controlled. The tighter the noose, the more they will resist. The battle itself can consume enormous amounts of organizational energy. The mavericks are slowly but surely surrounded, bounded, and hounded until there is no escape. They are locked up, like Jack Nicholson 's character in *One Flew Over the Cuckoo's Nest*.

This assault is also driven by fear. Who are these mavericks? Just what are they up to? Why don't they act "normal"? Why do they keep upsetting apple carts? Why can't they just get along? Once we have decided what "normal" is, everything else seems strange and even terrifying. We have to rid ourselves of it. "New opinions are always suspected, and usually opposed," wrote English philosopher John Locke, "without any other reason but because they are not already common."

This assault is often given credibility by the fact that the mavericks often express their opinions in anger and frustration, partly because they have their own shadow side and partly because they can sense that their opinions are unwelcome and probably have already been labeled as "wrong." Their anger puts the leery leader on the defensive, and so he or she comes after them even harder, so they respond in even more anger . . . around and around, chicken and egg.

So we build tools of conformity. We build balls and chains and tie them around the mavericks' legs. When the mavericks resist, we add more weight to the balls and more links to the chains.

These tools are killers of passion. They're horrible and terrible and deadly and ugly, but they "work" (they slow the mavericks down), so we keep using them. They squeeze out the originality and uniqueness and specialness. These tools lead to fear: fear to innovate, fear to try new things, fear to make mistakes. The mavericks give up and slowly die. As Vince Lombardi, the great football coach, said, "Once you learn to quit, it becomes a habit."

If you find people who have been in the workforce for five or ten years or more and are still constructive mavericks, pay them as much as you can. Do whatever it takes to keep them.

If life hasn't beaten the passion out of them, they're one in a thousand.

Safety for Risk Takers

But we need more than mavericks. They are too hard to find and too hard to keep. We need a lot of people who are simply willing to think about issues and express their opinions in a positive way.

We don't want to just make room for mavericks. We want a culture in which it is safe—no, *encouraged*—for people to try new things and take some risks. The first and biggest risk is a personal one: Will I expose myself? Will I dare to be me? Will I be willing to disagree? What will happen to me if I do? Will I be ridiculed? Ostracized? Terminated? These aren't idle questions. Most of us have spent a lifetime watching mavericks get beaten down by the system, and we're not sure the system will treat us any better. Simply expressing opinions can appear to be the biggest mistake of all.

This personal risk is greater in our minds than any risk to the organization's fortunes. We have to start at this point with our people. Telling them that we can afford their mistakes is insufficient; it's the wrong answer. We need to convince them that *they* can afford their mistakes. "Far better to dare mighty things, to win glorious triumphs, even though checkered by failure," said U.S. president Theodore Roosevelt, "than to take rank with those poor spirits who neither enjoy much nor suffer much, because they live in the gray twilight that knows not victory, nor defeat."

People talk about growing leaders, and that is a worthy goal. But true leaders don't come out of a box of cereal. Leaders are, by definition, people who are willing to get out in front, to be different, to set the pace. In other words, leaders are mavericks, if they are real leaders and not just figureheads. So the primary mission isn't to grow leaders, it's to grow *mavericks*.

And we don't want a maverick-friendly culture. We want a maverick-*hungry* culture, a maverick-*producing* culture. We want all of our people, no matter how quietly they do it, to differ from the group when it is off base, to dissent from its decisions, to be independent enough to think for themselves and not let someone else do it for them. "Leaders must create cultures in which experiments, questions, and challenges are not just for the courageous. The goal should be not to encourage more risk-taking but to make it less risky to create something that departs from convention."[5]

How do we do this?

• *We are reality-friendly.* While most organizations are reality-impaired, we embrace reality even when it hurts us or scares us. We encourage everyone to constantly question our theory of the business, our presuppositions, our assumptions, our structures, and our systems. Perception is not reality. We will find reality and embrace it.

• *We are truth-friendly.* We converse in such a way that people can hear us "thinking out loud," can know what our assumptions and doubts and questions as well as our certainties are. This will show them how to do it and teach them that it is appropriate, that it doesn't bring punishment. We know that there is no substitute for honesty mixed with vulnerability.

• *We are dissension-friendly.* We refuse to exert pressure for consensus. Consensus makes a very bad goal. Why is it important that we all totally agree with this decision or action (or at least pretend that we agree)? We tell ourselves that consensus is important in order to get buy-in, but even when people all say they agree, the level of buy-in extends over a broad range. It's more important, for both the quality of the decision *and* the buy-in, that people speak their mind and go forward with respect (their own and others') for their doubts, and perhaps with their disagreements intact. It is impossible to get complete consensus from complex beings on very complex issues. The very effort tends to breed silence and conformity.

- *We are risk-friendly.* We welcome ideas and actions that have a different perspective or take a different approach. We call it "innovation," not "going outside the rules."

- *We are mistake-friendly.* We refuse to allow anyone to be chastised or punished for making an honest mistake (one that was made without evil intent). This means no public criticism, no demotions, no terminations. We walk the talk. We say that mistakes are the way to creativity and growth, and we act like it.

- *We are noise-friendly.* We *do* punish silence. When we find that someone had a different idea and chose not to share it—*whether or not the idea was better*—we make it into a big deal. We let the person know that we can't believe it. How could you hold your tongue when you had a different thought? Do you think we're hiring you just to fill a job description? What on earth possessed you to say nothing? We've got to get across to all of our people that it is false and hidden consensus, not true and open conflict, that we really loathe and dread.

- *We are input-friendly.* We evaluate people, and have 360-degree feedback, to determine their willingness to speak up. We invite ideas on how to open up our culture, and we act on them. We assure everyone that they are invited to give us all of their opinions, even on issues outside their area.

Only when virtually everyone in our organization really believes that there is no risk to being honest will we truly have a passionate organization.

Conclusion

The problem is this: Either we take some minor pain along the way, or we get the really big pain down the road.

The reality is that we are all stumbling around in the dark. No one has a clear idea of what the economy or customers or people will be like in five or ten years. But we know things will be different. "All is change; all yields its place and goes," wrote the Greek tragedian Euripides in the 5th century B.C. The buzz saw of change is coming at us, ready or not, like it or not. We can ignore it and be cut down, or take hold of it and use it to clear a field for planting a new crop.

So we have a choice. We can stand still in the dark and take no chances on stubbing our toes. Hiding will feel good (or at least pain-less) for a while. We'll get a little nervous when we hear the buzz of the saw getting closer, but we are risk-averse, maverick-averse, honesty-averse, so we'll stand where we are and hope it will miss us.

But it won't miss us, because the saw is as big as the room. Change has always swallowed up the status quo, whatever it is. The only way to succeed is to get out of this dark room and go into the light. We'll have to start moving. And when we do, we're going to bang up against things that we didn't know were in the room. Some customers will complain or even leave us. We'll lose some money. We'll allocate some scarce resources to some dead ends. We'll make some false starts and a lot of mistakes, but we'll be moving. We'll find our way out of the room. The buzz saw won't destroy us.

We'll have some short-term pain, but we'll still have our legs.

Notes

1. *Hamlet*, 1.5.166.
2. Ecclesiastes 11:8, *The New International Version*.
3. Excerpted from *The American Heritage Dictionary of the English Language, Third Edition*. (Boston: Houghton Mifflin Company, 1996).
4. As quoted in *Forbes*, November 16, 1998, p. 106.
5. Rosabeth Moss Kanter, *On the Frontiers of Management* (Boston: Harvard Business School Press, 1997), p. 9.

18

Use Crises and Obstacles to Increase Passion

GM continued to display a dangerous reluctance to seriously engage its creative energies and resources in response to these issues. They were seen only as obstacles, not as fresh opportunities for new thinking. What, I wondered, was there to be creative about in the absence of obstacles?

—Jerry Hirshberg, *The Creative Priority*

It is in times of difficulty that great nations, like great men, display the whole energy of their character and become an object of admiration to posterity.

—Napoleon Bonaparte, *Maxims*

It still holds true that man is most uniquely human when he turns obstacles into opportunities.

—Eric Hoffer, *Reflections on the Human Condition*

The passionate organization isn't intimidated by change—it eats it as a regular diet. This organization unleashes the powers of its people to *exploit* change, even when it comes in the form of crisis or a major obstacle.

For many reasons, we humans tend to illude that our lives and work will go on in a smooth, comfortable, interesting, nontraumatic way for as far into the future as we can see or imagine. We expect nothing to change, unless *we* initiate the change.

But there are countless variables, most of which are not under our control in even the slightest degree, that can affect our efforts in ways that at first blush are tough, horrible, or even disastrous. Customers, suppliers, and partners can change their minds, change their needs, or simply go out of business. Key employees can make huge mistakes, waste resources, or simply go away. Laws can change, creating whole new traps and devouring resources. The good performance of most divisions can be negatively affected by the poor performance of one or two (for example, lack of profits in one division may cause the sale of a profitable division).

The biggest impacter of all, the marketplace—the sum of billions of individual and organizational decisions—is incomprehensible in its details, no matter what the prognosticators say. When the economy is healthy, companies invest, spend, hire, and promote—but not evenly. And when the economy is sick, companies postpone investments, reduce spending, and stop hiring and promoting—but not evenly. Our ability to anticipate is always limited.

So the crises will come. We will report earnings at or above estimated levels, and our stock price will immediately and remarkably drop five points. We will spend a lot of energy developing a new product or service based on our customers' input, and then they won't buy it. We will make an acquisition or develop an alliance that rings sweet and true, and the blasted thing will become a continual source of grief and pain. We will develop an outstanding plan for the future, and someone we never heard of will blow it away with a new idea or technology.

The obstacles will be even more frequent, even more prevalent, than the crises. Obnoxious customers, recalcitrant employees, inner turf wars that won't be erased by proclamations of "boundarylessness," technology snafus, quality problems, incentive programs that produce resentment rather than inspiration—all are part and parcel of being alive and being a leader in a complex organization. Winston Churchill said that "even ordinary life and business involve the encountering of unknown factors and require some effort of the imagination, some stress of the soul, to overcome them."

So the big question really isn't, really can't be, "How do we avoid crises and obstacles?" This is a good question, one worth wrestling with whenever we're looking at a new direction, idea, or plan. There are many things that can be anticipated and prevented, at least in part. Too few organizations really ask and answer this question in advance. The reality for the next century is heart *over* head, not heart *in lieu of* head. Passion is the driver, but we can't let it take us where it isn't smart to go.

The problem is that once a project gets rolling, it develops a bandwagon effect. Once we've made an emotional commitment to the project, we tend to see all of its roses and none of its thorns. We have to develop two disciplines: First, we have to ask and answer this question fully before we make an emotional commitment; and second, we have to ask it again and systematically *after* we've made an emotional commitment.

But an even bigger question is, "How will we exploit the inevitable crises and obstacles?" We need to develop an organizational mindset that understands that crises and obstacles will come, then emotionally prepare for them *even where no rational preparedness is possible*. We know they're coming. We won't be blown away by them. Bring them on.

What Crises and Obstacles Reveal

Crises and obstacles bring pressure. Few things in life are more revealing than pressure. "Adversity is the first path to Truth," wrote Lord Byron. Our organizations are like a car in idle until they are challenged. The challenge helps us see what we are made of.

How will we respond to the pressure? Will we rise to new heights? Or will we crack and crumble? Crises and obstacles reveal many things about us and our organizations:

• *Our character.* Our flaws will be brought out by pressure. We preach kindness, but we find ourselves snapping at others in meetings. We preach powersharing, but we find ourselves absorbing all the decision-making power. We preach a policy of openness, but we find ourselves holing up and avoiding people. The responses are normal and understandable; refusing to respond in these ways is extraordinary.

• *Our relationships.* Pressure shows us the quality, the depth, and the strength of our relationships. Is our information sharing real, or does it fade in crises? Do we really trust her, or do we find ourselves hedging on our powersharing with her? In the face of his big mistake, do we give him room to try again? When human error is the apparent cause of a crisis, continuing to give our trust is a very difficult and exceptional response.

• *The quality of our ideas.* This revelation comes in two forms. First, pressure tests the essential quality of our products, services, systems, and processes. Do they measure up? Are they ready for war? And second, pressure tests their staying power. Are they strong enough to endure? Are they flexible enough to meet unexpected demands? Few things are as fine, or as rare, as a leader who is willing to stay on the ship while others are jumping off, or a leader who is willing to abandon ship when many believe it will not sink.

• *Missing pieces.* Every idea has flaws. There are no perfect plans. Pressure reveals clearly where we are missing wisdom, truth, knowledge, information, data, or passion. It provides an opportunity to fill in the gaps, stop the game until we can learn the rules, or quit the game entirely. The usual response is to scapegoat: Who messed up our plan? The classier and passionate response is to grow: How do we find what we're missing?

• *Our illusions.* Pressure reveals more than just what we are missing. It also reveals "what we know that just ain't so."[1] Every idea is based to some degree on assumptions and presuppositions and perceptions. It is far too easy for one or more of these to be disconnected from reality. Pressure gives us the opportunity to revisit our framework and abandon our illusions, some of which are cherished and many of which can be fatal.[2] "Radical shedding happens in the crises that move in on the soul and cannot be easily fixed," says James Hillman.[3]

• *Our beliefs.* Pressure lets us know what we really believe and are willing to fight for. If the idea is fundamentally sound, if we know it's critical to our future success, will we stick to it in the face of ugly early returns?

The best response when a crisis or major obstacle comes is to ask the question, "What is this telling us? What can we learn?"

It beats wringing our hands or looking for someone to blame.

Understanding Responses to Change

Passion is a key ingredient, perhaps *the* key ingredient, in responding effectively to change, before or at the time it reaches crisis proportions. Our rational side sees all the reasons why we will be devoured. Our passionate side stirs our soul to fight for victory. Let's take a look at the different ways organizations respond to change and the amount of passion involved in each of these situations.

- *Dying organizations* choose to be blind. They can't see the change even when it is obvious. Their people have no passion and spend their lives just putting in time. Their attitude is, "It all pays the same." They're the people who ask, "What happened?" Too many people live here.

- *Passive organizations* don't change even when the need is obvious and they feel the pain. Their people have only a little passion. Instead, they rely on magical thinking and hope things will get better. They respond to the pain by being upset and asking, "Whose fault is this?" This is the all-too-common first response to crises.

- *Reactionary organizations* respond to change, but only after the pain has reached crisis proportions. Their only passion is to survive. They have little motivation to think about and restructure for the long term, so they find themselves with limited time and resources to react. They ask, "Can we make it through?" They usually takes desperate measures, while turning from a "fast follower" to a "fast casualty."

- *Anticipatory organizations* see change coming, prepare for it, and consider it an opportunity. They have enough passion to thrive. They unleash people and projects in many directions, and provide ample time and resources to take advantage of change. "How can we exploit this?" they ask. They are nascent passionate organizations, ready to turn obstacles and crises to their advantage. "The ability to adapt to different conditions is the most telling measure of success for any organization."[4]

- *Creative organizations* initiate change and consider it a competitive advantage. They are the ultimate passionate organizations. They keep people shaken out of routine and the status quo. They get there first because they're setting the pace. "Where will the action be?" they ask. They view crises and obstacles as opportunities to learn and grow. Passionate organizations anticipate and create change. And they use crises and obstacles as opportunities to increase passion.

Using Crises and Obstacles to Increase Passion

How does the passionate organization use apparent disasters and problems to increase passion?

- *Shake up the status quo.* The easiest approach for any organization is to settle in, get comfortable, and eventually get stuck. And we can get just as stuck by success as by average performance or mediocrity. "Crises and deadlocks when they occur have at least this advantage, that they force us to think," said Indian Prime Minister Jawaharlal Nehru. Passionate organizations view problems as a means of pruning the garbage growth so that the tree will grow to its full height and potential.

- *Use problems as stepping-stones.* Where do we go from here? How do we get our future jump-started? Most organizations flounder when they encounter problems. Passionate organizations use them as stepping-stones into the future. Here is pain. What's the cure? They use a passion-driven, reason-supported process that looks like this:

1. Acknowledge the presence, impact, and severity of the problem.
2. Define the problem accurately, concisely, and at the deepest level in both emotional and rational terms.
3. Conduct a broad, open-ended, and no-holds-barred analysis of the problem, its causes, and its drivers.
4. Passionately brainstorm and explore multiple, diverse, and out-of-the-box solutions.
5. Synthesize a better-than-all-alternatives solution that does more than simply solve the problem.
6. Develop a timely, passionately-supported, and understandable implementation plan.
7. Optimize the solution through monitoring, measurement, and mid-course corrections as appropriate, or discard it and go back to step 1.

- *Beware the shadow.* We can spend vast amounts of energy on problems and make them our focus. We can assign our best people and other resources to dealing with them. Most organizations do this very thing. But passionate organizations make *solutions* and *outgrowth opportunities* their focus, not the problems themselves. Their passion is for growth, not just for problem solving.

- *Play off opposition.* Opposition is critical to growth. Few teams ever reach their highest potential unless they have the strong opposition of an impossible deadline, unjust criticism, or a fierce and relentless competitor. Passionate organizations can't live without opposition. If it doesn't occur naturally in their environment, they will invent it.[5]

- *Value complaints.* "Most companies treat customer complaints . . . as dreaded plagues. . . . Companies would be better-served by viewing customer complaints as a source of strategic opportunity. . . . Complaints and complainers often are more valuable to you than plans and planners."[6] Passionate organizations are thrilled to find out how they have failed. They seek out complaints as a friend. They recognize employees who uncover the most, or the most interesting, complaints.

- *Use creativity as a weapon.* Most organizations respond to problems with panic. Passionate organizations respond to problems with patience. They know that this is the time to sit and brainstorm their way out of the mine field rather than to simply start running. This is the time to act both rationally ("we *can* win") and passionately ("we *will* win"). Creativity is the "marriage of passion and logic."[7]

- *Welcome friendly fire.* What do we do when the obstacles are our own people? Most organizations silence internal opposition. This is considered good and healthy business practice. But passionate organizations welcome it, encourage it, invite it, nourish it. They would rather hear about the pending crisis from a friend than from an enemy, from a member of the organizational family than from a stranger. They lay everything out before their people and ask, "Where are we off or missing something?" rather than, "Do you like and agree with this?" "It is a three phase process," Ted Harris, UPIU union local president at Harley Davidson, told me. "There is the before, the during, and the after. In a high-performance work organization, you want input from everyone during all three phases. Rather than things being dictated, you can say, 'Look at what we have done and how much better it is going to be.'"

Conclusion

The future is not a given. It isn't predetermined. It will be what we and many other people make of it. Negotiating it effectively is much more a matter of responding well emotionally than of planning well rationally. The passionate organization creates many possible paths to the future and unleashes people on all paths about which they are passionate.

And, when the certain-to-come crises and obstacles arrive, to be ready to take them on with a roar.

Notes

1. Kin Hubbard, American humorist.
2. For a thorough treatment of the critical leadership skill of thrashing illusions and grasping reality, see my book *Fatal Illusions: Shredding a Dozen Unrealities That Can Keep Your Organization From Success* (New York: AMACOM, 1997).
3. James Hillman, *Kinds of Power* (New York: Currency Doubleday, 1995), p. 55.
4. Bruce Pasternak and Albert J. Viscio, *The Centerless Corporation* (New York: Simon & Shuster, 1998), p. 44.
5. For a discussion of dealing effectively with adversity, see Paul G. Stoltz, *The Adversity Quotient* (New York: John Wiley & Sons, Inc., 1997).
6. Oren Harari, "Thank Heavens for Complainers," *Management Review*, March 1997, p. 25.
7. Jerry Hirshberg, *The Crative Priority: Driving Innovative Business in the Real World* (New York: HarperBusiness, 1998), p. 194.

19

Spiritual Leadership in Secular Places

There's one more item on our list of Things Leaders Must Do, and it's just what your broker says Investors Must Not Do: fall in love. There are CEOs who slash and CEOs who fix and CEOs who safeguard and CEOs who build. The great ones do all these things too, but first of all they love. Passion, commitment, ferocity—the traits of lovers are in these leaders.

—Thomas A. Stewart in *Fortune* magazine

Twixt kings and tyrants there's this difference known: Kings seek their subjects' good, tyrants their own.

—Robert Herrick, *Hesperides*

Every CEO has to be a cheerleader.

—Richard A. Zimmerman, CEO, Hershey Foods

No more small leaders.

Only one kind of leader can lead a passionate organization. All of us who lead others, whether we have a title or not, need a fundamental shift in thinking to see ourselves as spiritual leaders. And we need to *be* that kind of leader.

People simply won't follow someone who isn't chasing a dream that's big and worthwhile. Spiritual leaders give direction to the fire. They turn up the heat all around them, a heat that sets others aflame.

They burn with a red-hot intensity that makes it easier for all to see the way to victory.

Seven Pillars of Spiritual Leadership in Secular Places

Regardless of their religious beliefs or doctrines, spiritual leaders—those who lead people in a particularly exalting way—have some key traits in common. Let's take a look together at seven attributes of spiritual leaders, wherever they are found. After that, we will address some of the things that spiritual leaders *don't* do.

1. *Spiritual leaders are focused on others first and themselves second.* There is no question that narcissistic leaders can generate great charisma and get some people to follow them—often those who themselves are narcissistic, or who want someone else to think and maybe even live for them. But spiritual leadership can't be faked. People will know almost instantly who the leader's object of affection is: them or himself. If we truly put others first, even when we are making the decision, even when we are getting the glory or rewards, people will follow us. Spiritual leaders are fiercely committed to their followers. "I have worked without thinking of myself," said A.P. Giannini, the founder of modern banking. "[This is] the largest factor in whatever success I have attained."[1]

Spiritual leaders make it a priority to be with their people, not because it's a duty or best practice, but because they really do believe those other people have transcendent value. "I can't do anything more important than get out on the floor," Karl Eberle, Harley-Davidson vice president, told me. "I love to be out on the floor, because on the floor I understand what the issues are and I can respond to them and I can also send these little messages. . . . I can have a tremendous impact on momentum. . . . They really believe that I care." He summarized his thoughts this way: "Relationships are the key to passion."

2. *Spiritual leaders are focused on organizational success rather than personal ambition.* "There is no limit to the amount of good that people can do if they don't care who gets the credit," says an old proverb.

Who does the leader talk about? Always the organization? Or always his or her own plans and goals? We have to get ourselves out of the way if we're going to lead people to higher and better places. The good news is that we will reach those higher and better places with them. A rising tide lifts all boats.

Spiritual leaders transfer real ownership to those who are passionate about the vision and values. They know that if people own something, they will believe in it and fight for it. And somehow, some way, they'll make it happen.

3. *Spiritual leaders are able to articulate people's dreams.* Most of our dreams from childhood and early adulthood are pretty well squelched by the time we have been working for a few years. But the dreams never completely go away. They lie dormant, waiting for someone to call them forth, to bring them back to life, to breathe on them and warm them. We can learn what those dreams and fragments of dreams are, not to manipulate people, but to draw from those dreams as deep wells. When we are talking their dreams, we are talking more than their language.

Spiritual leaders love to teach, by word and example and mostly by parable. They tell stories, encourage others to tell stories, and develop forums and mechanisms for all great stories about vision and values to be told. They know that stories are the best way to communicate the most difficult concepts and complex ideas. They believe in the vision so strongly that they teach it passionately, even evangelistically, so that others can believe in it as well. They entice people by using their own dreams as the lure. They remind people of what is special about themselves, and how that is valued by the organization. Spiritual leaders know the music that is inside their people, and play it for them when they forget.

4. *Spiritual leaders are willing to give guidance but avoid taking control.* Spiritual leaders don't keep what they know to themselves. Regardless of what it has cost them to learn it, they give it away for free. They care about other people too much to let them make avoidable mistakes. They delight in others' successes rather than their failures.

But they don't use their wisdom and experience as tools of control. They give both the advice to be followed and the freedom not to follow it. No one will ever be controlled to greatness, and spiritual leaders know this in their souls.

Spiritual leaders strive to expand leadership to all who are willing to care. "Leaders must be willing to lose control," Michael Mahoney, president of Manufacturing Decision Analysis, told me. "Loss of control . . . is not a threat but an opportunity . . . to attain superior levels of knowledge and performance previously not considered." Spiritual leaders take time to understand what people's real issues are.

5. *Spiritual leaders are willing to champion causes or needs.* Most leaders stockpile power to use to their own advantage or to the advantage of their "turf." Spiritual leaders use any accumulated power to fight for good things and true things and needed things and impossible, lost causes. Their first question isn't, "How will this make me look?" but rather, "How much good will this do?" They know that on their deathbeds, personal power has a net present worth of zero, whereas spent power can create value for generations.

Spiritual leaders are enthusiastic. They shape people's attitudes and opinions and passions with their enthusiasm, which draws people in with a powerful and magnetic force. Spiritual leaders are willing to be childlike in exhibiting their unrestrained excitement and joy. They are somehow able to lay aside worries about how they will be perceived or whether their dignity will suffer.

You can see the passion even when a spiritual leader is making a formal presentation. When asked about the main problem CEOs had in making such presentations, high-level coach Trudi Bresner answered, "Demonstrating commitment and passion."[2]

6. *Spiritual leaders have integrity in words and actions in all phases of their lives.* They don't live lives of integrity just so that they won't be caught. They live this way because they know that internal consistency enhances their power and maximizes their chances of getting things done. They don't have to worry about what they told to whom and when. They can focus relentlessly on their vision. When leaders preach charity but give nothing, preach morality but use others, preach trust but look over shoulders, they have ceased to be spiritual leaders and have instead become bad examples.

Spiritual leaders don't buy into the debate about public versus private character. They believe it is nonsense to say that a person can be a rogue in private life but a role model at the helm. They also know the difference between character, which is what you do in the dark, and reputation, an ephemeral commodity that is not under their control. Their focus is on character.

7. *Spiritual leaders have a balance of confidence and humility.* Spiritual leaders have the certainty that they are supposed to be leading combined with the certainty that they are fallible. They know that leadership isn't a blank check, that just because they are leaders doesn't mean that their thinking is always clear or their decisions always right.

They are marked by their sense of pilgrimage, their sense that they are on a long journey where what they receive and give along the way really matters. They don't think that they've "arrived," and they don't see retirement as an end. They are fascinated by the process of life.

None of these pillars is unattainable by anyone who desires to be one of these most outstanding of leaders. Even if we have failed at some or all of these points in the past, we can start today and really become spiritual leaders.

What Spiritual Leaders Don't Do

There are some paths that spiritual leaders won't take under any circumstances.

* *Spiritual leaders never treat the organization in a cavalier manner.* They don't create rapid expansion followed by brutal downsizing. They don't make across-the-board cuts, where the productive get cut equally with the unproductive. And they don't push quality one quarter and cost cutting the next, running the organization on the depleting method of "initiatives."

* *Spiritual leaders never allow gaps.* They don't permit communication gaps, widely disparate wage gaps, or participation gaps. They brook no "have" and "have-not" thinking. Their focus is always on connection—between people, between departments, between divisions, between inside and outside people, between us and our stakeholders. They believe that relationship is the key, and they won't let it be compromised.

* *Spiritual leaders never use fear.* They never use fear or allow it to be used by others. They know that fear works, and that's one of the reasons they hate it so much. They believe that fear is the lowest common denominator of bad leaders and ugly micromanagers. If spiritual leaders can't get someone to do it without making him or her

afraid, they find someone else who is motivated by nobler reasons. And they listen for any sign of organizational stories that illustrate a reign of terror.

Conclusion

Human beings are not motivated by facts, no matter how compelling; they are motivated by stories that affect their emotions. Passionate organizations are driven by stories, which are woefully lacking in rational organizations.

Spiritual leaders make the "story"—whether told by them, told by others, or shared by those affected in companywide meetings—the primary driving force for change and growth. Leaders, in fact, will themselves have to embody the story and live it out in a public way with integrity.

The future, as GE's Jack Welch reminds us, will belong to "passionate, driven leaders—people who not only have enormous energy, but who can energize those whom they lead."

Organizations desperately need the fire of employee commitment. The spiritual leader has the means to ignite that fire.

Notes

1. As quoted in *Time*, December 7, 1998, p. 94.
2. As quoted in "Making Over CEOs," *Fortune*, September 7, 1998, p. 144.

Epilogue

The Triumph of the Passionate Organization

There is only one big thing—desire. And before it, when it is big, all is little.

—Novelist Willa Cather

Nothing splendid was ever created in cold blood. Heat is required to forge anything. Every great accomplishment is the story of a flaming heart.

—Arnold Glascow

It is unfortunate that many organizations find themselves on the yellow brick road: searching for a brain, searching for a heart, and searching for courage.

—R. Michael Mahoney
President, Manufacturing Decision Analysis LLC

We live in a day when leaders in many organizations are realizing that the game is people and the formula for winning it is involvement.

This has led many on a search for a way of navigating the shoals that make up the fuzzy landscape of the twenty-first century. The quest has indeed put them on the yellow brick road, looking for:

- *A brain.* We live in a knowledge economy, and our people have to be knowledge workers. Without the full utilization of their minds, we're in deep trouble. We need to be learning organizations and teaching organizations, accumulating vast quantities of information and then doing something useful with it. We need to look inside and find an intelligent organization.

• *A heart.* We live in an economy in which the competition is rough and competitive advantages are really hard to come by. It isn't as easy to see, but we also live in an emotional economy, and our people have to be passionate workers. Without the full utilization of their hearts, we're finished. We need to be visionary organizations, trusting organizations, accumulating many ways to make a difference and building them into greater goals. We need to look inside and find a passionate organization.

• *Courage.* We have to believe that we can win this game if we find a way into the vast resources inside the incredible and amazing—and sometimes shockingly disappointing—people with whom we work. We have to go where leaders in a calmer age did not have to venture. It was enough for them to tap into the minds of a few, the time of the many, and nobody's heart but their own. That day is gone. It takes courage to face it, and courage to win with the new requirements. "Knowledge changes, but passion is a constant," says Pfizer.

The passionate organization. The possibility of building and leading one is there before us.

And with it, triumph.

• • •

Thank you for letting me share a bit of the ride with you. If you would like to contact me with a thought or question, to tell me about what you're doing—or intend to do—to build a passionate organization, I'd love to hear from you. You can reach me at:

James R. Lucas, President
Luman Consultants
P.O. Box 2566
Shawnee Mission, KS 66201
(Kansas City area)
Telephone: 913-248-1733
Fax: 913-671-7728
E-mail: JLucasLC@aol.com

I'll do my best to get you a timely (and passionate) reply.

Bibliography

Belasco, James A., and Ralph C. Stayer. *Flight of the Buffalo: Soaring to Excellence, Learning to Let Employees Lead* (New York: Warner Books, 1993).

Bennis, Warren, and Patricia Ward Biederman. *Organizing Genius: The Secrets of Creative Collaboration* (Reading, Mass.: Addison-Wesley Publishing Company, Inc., 1997).

Bernstein, Peter L. *Against the Gods: The Remarkable Story of Risk* (New York: John Wiley & Sons, Inc., 1997).

Brown, Thomas L. *The Anatomy of Fire* (www.mgeneral. com), 1997.

Collins, James C., and Jerry I. Porras. *Built to Last: Successful Habits of Visionary Companies* (New York: HarperBusiness, 1994).

Drucker, Peter F. *Managing in a Time of Great Change* (New York: Truman Talley Books, 1995).

Fitz-Enz, Jac. *The 8 Practices of Exceptional Companies: How Great Organizations Make the Most of Their Human Assets* (New York: AMACOM, 1997).

Freiberg, Kevin L., and Jacquelyn A. Freiberg. *Nuts! Southwest Airlines' Crazy Recipe for Business and Personal Success* (New York: Bard Press, 1996).

Goleman, Daniel. *Working With Emotional Intelligence* (New York: Bantam, 1998).

Gubman, Edward L. *The Talent Solution: Aligning Strategy and People to Achieve Extraordinary Results* (New York: McGraw-Hill, 1998).

Handy, Charles. *The Hungry Spirit* (New York: Broadway Books, 1998).

Harris, Jim. *Getting Employees to Fall In Love With Your Company* (New York: AMACOM, 1996).

Hirshberg, Jerry. *The Creative Priority: Driving Innovative Business in the Real World* (New York: HarperBusiness, 1998).

Kanter, Rosabeth Moss. *On the Frontiers of Management* (Boston: Harvard Business School Press, 1997).

Lee, William G. *Mavericks in the Workplace: Harnessing the Genius of American Workers* (New York: Oxford University Press, 1998).

Lucas, James R. *Balance of Power* (New York: AMACOM, 1998).

Lucas, James R. *Fatal Illusions: Shredding a Dozen Unrealities That Can Keep Your Organization From Success* (New York: AMACOM, 1997).

Mintzberg, Henry. *The Rise and Fall of Strategic Planning* (New York: The Free Press, 1994).

Pasternak, Bruce A., and Albert J. Viscio. *The Centerless Corporation* (New York: Simon & Schuster, 1998).

Sanders, T. Irene. *Strategic Thinking and the New Science: Planning in the Midst of Chaos, Complexity, and Change* (New York: The Free Press, 1998).

Simmons, Annette. *Territorial Games: Understanding and Ending Turf Wars at Work* (New York: AMACOM, 1998).

Tichy, Noel M. *The Leadership Engine: How Winning Companies Build Leaders at Every Level* (New York: HarperBusiness, 1997).

Tobin, Daniel R. *The Knowledge-Enabled Organization: Moving from "Training" to "Learning"* (New York: AMACOM, 1998).

Useem, Michael. *The Leadership Moment: Nine True Stories of Truimph and Disaster and Their Lessons for Us All* (New York: Times Business, 1998).

Zohar, Danah. *Rewiring the Corporate Brain* (New York: Berrett-Koehler Publishers, 1997).

Index

Other Reading By James R. Lucas

Leadership and Organizational Development:

Balance of Power
Fatal Illusions: Shredding a Dozen Unrealities That Can Keep Your Organization From Success

Family and Other Relationships:
1001 Ways to Connect With Your Kids
Proactive Parenting: The Only Approach That Really Works
The Parenting of Champions

Personal Life and Growth:
Walking Through the Fire

Fiction:
Voyage to a New Earth
Weeping in Ramah